TABLE OF CONTENTS

Hangang 한강 - A Riverside Playground for All!

8 SPOTS   6 ACTIVITIES   2 CHALLENGES

Flowing through the heart of the city, Hangang provides a serene escape from urban hustle. Embrace stunning views, cultural events, and recreational activities. From relaxing strolls to enjoyable picnics, Hangang offers something for all, creating cherished and unforgettable moments for every visitor.

Royal Palaces of Seoul - Discover the Gems of Korean History

36 SPOTS   38 ACTIVITIES   13 CHALLENGES

The five royal palaces of Seoul boast stunning architecture, immaculate gardens, and fascinating historical significance that will transport you back in time, providing a glimpse into Korea's rich and captivating history. Additionally, you can partake in enjoyable cultural activities like wearing traditional hanbok clothing and watching traditional performances. Moreover, make sure to visit Cheong Wa Dae, the former residence of South Korean presidents, now open to the public, offering a breathtaking view from the surrounding Bugaksan mountain.

Hanok Villages - Step Back in Time and Experience Korean Lifestyle

9 SPOTS   8 ACTIVITIES   5 CHALLENGES

Experience the unique beauty of traditional Korean architecture as you wander through the streets of these historic neighborhoods. Immerse yourself in the traditional Korean way of life and gain a deeper understanding of the country's rich culture and heritage. These villages offer a glimpse into Korea's past with their charming cafes, local shops, and stunning architectural details.

Korean Street Food Showdown - Enjoy Korea's Most Beloved Street Eats!

5 SPOTS   5 ACTIVITIES   2 CHALLENGES

Indulge in the authentic flavors of Korean street eateries and immerse yourself in the vibrant atmosphere where locals gather to savor their favorite dishes. Experience the true essence of local dining, just like a local resident!

Souvenir Shopping - Take a Piece of Korea Home

5 SPOTS **3 ACTIVITIES** **6 CHALLENGES**

Seoul's vibrant souvenir shops and flea markets offer an incredible selection of unique and traditional Korean souvenirs. From traditional crafts to modern trinkets, these shops offer something for everyone.

Gangnam Style - Explore Korea's Trendiest District!

16 SPOTS **38 ACTIVITIES** **13 CHALLENGES**

Immerse yourself in the vibrant culture of Gangnam, the trendiest and fashionable part of Seoul, through a variety of fun activities and experiences. From trying out the latest K-beauty trends to indulging in delicious local cu

K-Pop Adventure - A Journey into the Korean Pop Music Scene!

11 SPOTS **3 ACTIVITIES** **6 CHALLENGES**

Take a journey through Korea's music scene, where you'll get an up-close and personal look at the industry that has taken the world by storm. Visit K-Pop entertainment companies, follow the footsteps of K-Pop stars, take photos with the iconic K-Pop bear statues, and even learn a few dance moves to experience what it's like to be a K-Pop idol!

Tragedies and Triumphs - Exploring Korea's History Through Museums

4 SPOTS **3 ACTIVITIES** **5 CHALLENGES**

Discover the amazing achievements of the past and learn about Korea's modern history and the struggles the nation faced. You'll hear both tragic stories and stories of victory that will leave you inspired and connected to the spirit of the Korean people. Jump on this unforgettable journey and celebrate the brilliance of the past and look forward to the future.

Finding Peace in Seoul - A Spiritual Journey to Calm the Mind and Body

8 SPOTS   **6 ACTIVITIES**   **6 CHALLENGES**

Delve into the heart of Korea's spiritual tapestry as you visit revered Buddhist temples, historic churches, and grand mosques. Immerse yourself in tranquil landscapes, embrace profound reflections, and find inner peace amidst cultural diversity.

Seoul Adventures - Family-Friendly and Romantic Activities for Everyone

17 SPOTS   **14 ACTIVITIES**   **21 CHALLENGES**

Whether you're a family looking to strengthen your bonds or a couple in search of romantic moments, Seoul has an abundance of excitement and unforgettable experiences for everyone. The city promises a delightful mix of family-friendly and intimate adventures that will surely create cherished memories to treasure.

Essential Apps and Books for Your Trip to KOREA

Subway Korea

Provides the latest subway map of Seoul and all subway maps provide real-time transit, timetable, transfer information, as well as an optimal route calculator.

Naver Map

From turn-by-turn directions to train schedules to nearby bathroom locations, this app provides everything you need for getting around Korea.

PAPAGO

This AI-based app provides superb translation especially in Korea, which is a must when you're traveling in Korea.

Catch Table

Lets you easily make restaurant reservations in English.

Kakao Map

Similar to Naver Map, but if you have Kakaot Talk, it's more handy as it's more closely integrated with other services like Kakao Taxi and Kakao Talk.

Google Maps

Similar to Naver Map, but lacks walking directions in Korea. Provides subway info and nearby places in more languages than Naver Map.

Emergency Ready

Offering quick access to nationwide shelters, emergency medical centers, fire stations, police stations, safety guides, and direct 119 emergency calls.

1330 Korea Travel Helpline

Offers voice call and live chat support for tourists, delivering travel info in 8 languages, assisting with interpretation, complaints, and accessing police assistance when needed.

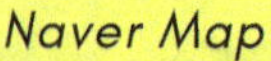

Seoul Korea Subway Tour Guide

Teaches you how to enjoy the city's top 100 attractions just by taking the subway.

Korean Culture Dictionary

Provides a comprehensive guide to Korea and its culture, from A to Z, enhancing your enjoyment of your trip to Korea.

Seoul Korea Restaurants & Cafes Guide by Real Locals

What to Eat, Where to Go, and How to Make Reservations with QR Code for a Seamless Dining Experience

MONEY IN KOREA

500 오백원
(O-BAEK-WON),
ROUGHLY 50 US CENTS

100 백원
(BAEK-WON),
ROUGHLY 10 US CENTS

50 오십원
(O-SHIP-WON),
ROUGHLY 5 US CENTS

10 십원
(SHIP-WON),
ROUGHLY 1 US CENT

MAJOR CREDIT CARDS
(VISA/MC/AMEX) ARE ACCEPTED
NEARLY EVERYWHERE IN KOREA,

SAMSUNG GALAXY PAY & APPLE
PAY ARE ALSO AVAILABLE

YOU CAN USE YOUR DEBIT CARD ISSUED IN YOUR OWN COUNTRY
TO WITHDRAW MONEY FROM AN ATM MACHINE IN KOREA.
LOOK FOR THE "GLOBAL ATM" SIGN ON AN ATM MACHINE.

T-MONEY CARD 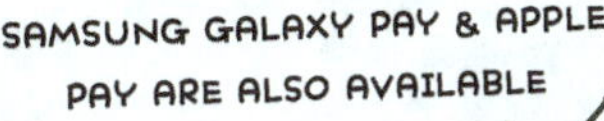

HAS TO BE PURCHASED AT AN OUTLET
BEARING THE T-MONEY LOGO, A
VENDING MACHINE (LINE 1-4), OR AT
THE INFORMATION CENTER INSIDE A
STATION (LINE 5-8).

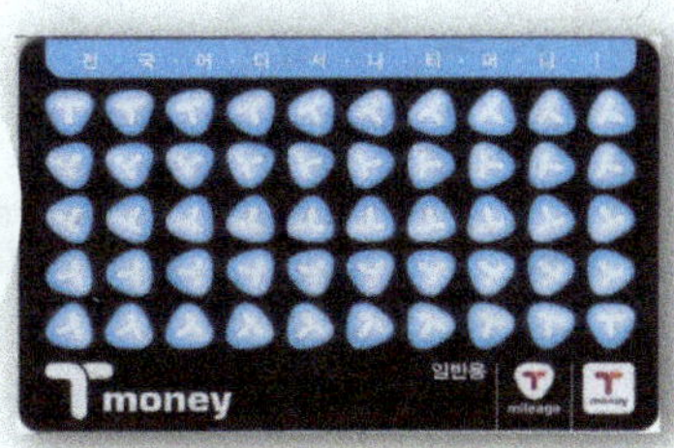

FOR SUBWAY / BUS / TAXI

Hangang 한강

A Riverside Playground for All!

Flowing through the heart of the city, Hangang provides a serene escape from urban hustle. Embrace stunning views, cultural events, and recreational activities. From relaxing strolls to enjoyable picnics, Hangang offers something for all, creating cherished and unforgettable moments for every visitor.

Hangang is a sprawling river that runs through various parts of the city, providing several access points for visitors. However, we will focus on **Banpo Hangang Park** since it offers a little something extra with its **Floating Island** and **Rainbow Bridge**. That said, choosing one over the other won't make much difference, as all of the spots offer a similar experience!

Banpo Hangang Park 반포 한강 공원 Seocho-gu, Shinbanpo-ro 11-gil 40 서초구 신반포로11길 40
25 minute walk (0.8 mi / 1.3 km) from **Express Bus Terminal Station Exit #8-1 Subway Line 9**

Yeouido Hangang Park 여의도 한강 공원 Yeongdeungpo-gu, Yeouidong-ro 330 영등포구 여의동로 330
5 minute walk (0.15 mi / 249 m) from **Yeouinaru Station Exit #3 Subway Line 5**

Ichon Hangang Park 이촌 한강 공원 Yongsan-gu, Ichon-dong 302-17 이촌동 302-17
20 minute walk (0.8 mi / 1.3 km) from **Ichon Station Exit #4 Subway Line 4**

Ttukseom Hangang Park 뚝섬 한강 공원 Gwangjin-gu, Jayang-dong 704-1 광진구 자양동 704-1
Right next to **Ttukseom Resort Station Exit #3 Subway Line 7**

Jamsil Hangang Park 잠실 한강 공원 Songpa-gu, Jamsil-dong 1-1 송파구 잠실동 1-
25 minute walk (0.9 mi / 1.5 km) from **Jamsil Station Exit #6 Subway Line 2**

Banpo Hangang Park 반포 한강 공원
Seocho-gu, Shinbanpo-ro 11-gil 40 서초구 신반포로11길 40
25 minute walk (0.8m / 1.3km) from **Express Bus Terminal Station Exit #8-1 Subway Line 9**

SCAN FOR DIRECTIONS!

① Let's Have a Picnic at Hangang!

You may bring your own tent, or there are many tent rental shops around the area for about $20. There are convenience stores and public restrooms nearby as well.

Allowed Season
Apr 1st - Oct 31

Hours
Apr - May, Sep - Oct
9 a.m. - 7 p.m

Jun - Aug
9 a.m. - 8 p.m.

Rental shops are located at Seocho-gu, Banpodaero 316, B1 **서초구 반포대로 316 지하 1층**
See the map above for reference ★

Savor the Chimaek (Chicken & Beer) Combo!

Chimaek 치맥 , which is short for "Chicken" + "*Maekju* 맥주 (beer)", is a popular choice for Korean picnickers. At **Seorae Naru 서래나루** , which is just a short walk from the Floating Island, there is a restaurant that specializes in chimaek and has a spacious seating area, so you don't have to go through the hassle of ordering and picking up delivery.

Try the Instant Ramyun Noodle Machine!

Visit a convenience store along the river, and find **a machine that prepares instant ramyun noodles!** All you have to do is put the noodles and soup into the designated container, and the machine will automatically dispense water and start cooking (if you are not sure, ask any Korean park visitor and they will be more than happy to help). **Savor your delicious ramyun noodle while admiring the stunning view of Hangang!**

제이 blog.naver.com/travelcrazykorean (CC BY-SA 2.0 KR)

Capture the Perfect Moment at Hangang's Best Photo Spots!

Look at the big full moon! People say that if you make a wish during the Super Moon and think about the rabbits that Koreans believe live on the moon in old stories, your wish might come true.

The crescent is a special symbol of Sebit Island! It looks nice in the daytime, but remember to enjoy its even prettier side at nighttime!

The stage outside in the middle of the square is where folks take group photos and do fun challenges for Social Media! Create your next viral video here!

② Visit the Futuristic Floating Island 세빛섬!

Boasting **a fantastic night view** where colorful and beautiful LED lights harmonize with the river, **Some Sevit 세빛섬 (Floating Island)** is one of Seoul's **most visited night spots**. It consists of artificial islands with wedding conventions, restaurants, and cafes and is used as a space for yachts, tube boats, and various exhibitions, performances, and events to enjoy.

*Sebit / Sevit, Gabit / Gavit, Solbit / Solvit are used interchangeably.

For more information, visit **somesevit.com**

In the movie **Avengers: Age of Ultron**, the Floating Island is referred to as **Sokovia**. The island was created by the villainous Ultron, who used it as a base for his evil plans!

Have a Mini Picnic on the River on a Tubester!

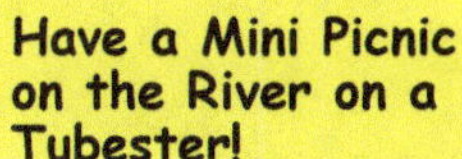

Enjoy a tranquil experience on your **private mini watercraft**, bring along your favorite food and drinks, and savor the serene beauty of nature surrounding you! Located on the **ground floor of Gabit Island**, it's the ideal spot for a **mini picnic on the river!**

Price:
30 mins: 35,000 won
60 mins: 55,000 won (per 1 boat)
Cash / Credit card accepted.

For safety, minors must be accompanied by an adult, and infants, pregnant women, elderly individuals, and those under 90cm (3 ft) tall are prohibited from using the service.

Capacity:
6 people max with a table

Hours:
Mar - May / Oct
Mon-Fri: 15:00 - 23:00
Sat/Sun/Holiday: 13:00 - 23:00
Jun - Sep
Mon-Fri: 16:00 - 24:00
Sat/Sun/Holiday: 14:00 - 24:00

"

3 Watch the Amazing Rainbow Fountain Bridge!

The park is home to the amazing **Banpo Bridge Rainbow Fountain - the world's longest bridge fountain that spans over 1,140 meters!** And the best part? At night, the fountain is lit up with vibrant LED lights, creating a magical water and light show that is absolutely mesmerizing! It's truly a sight to behold! And yes! **It's adjacent to the picnic zone**, so you can enjoy the spectacle with your picnic buddies!

	Duration	Operating Hours
May-Jun	20 min	12 p.m, 7:30 p.m., 8 p.m., 8:30 p.m., 9:00 p.m.
Jul-Aug	20 min	12 p.m, 7:30 p.m., 8 p.m., 8:30 p.m., 9:00 p.m., 9:30 p.m.
Sep-Oct	20 min	12 p.m, 7:30 p.m., 8 p.m., 8:30 p.m., 9:00 p.m.

Note: Fountain operations may be suspended due to weather conditions such as rainstorms or strong winds.

4 Beat the Heat at the Moonlight Night Market!

홍대 준게스트하우스 blog.naver.com/juny-house (CC BY-ND 2.0 KR)

Experience a unique and delightful evening at the **Hangang Moonlight Market** held at **Banpo Hangang Park (Moonlight Square)**. With food **trucks and craft artists** participating, the market offers a wide variety of delicious treats for visitors to enjoy.

Hangang Moonlight Market @ Banpo Hangang Park

Venue: Moonlight Square
Merchants: 40 food trucks, 50 booths
Schedule: 4 p.m. –9 p.m. (Sunday Only) from May 7 to Jun.11, 2023

Hangang Moonlight Market @ YeouidoHangang Park

Venue: Cascade Plaza
Merchants: 40 food trucks, 50 booths
Schedule: 5 p.m. –10 p.m. (Saturday & Sunday) from Sep.16 to Oct.22, 2023

For more information, visit **bamdokkaebi.org**

Pedal along the Scenic Hangang with Seoul Bike!

Hangang is the perfect destination for a fun-filled day of **biking and sightseeing!** With **designated bike trails stretching 240 km along the river,** you can enjoy stunning views and catch glimpses of locals and tourists alike.

bikeseoul.com

With **Seoul Bike** (*tta-reung-i* 따릉이 in Korean), you can easily join in on the fun and rent a bike for an affordable price. The service can be accessed **online** or through their **mobile app**. Real-time information on bike availability can be found on their map, with **bike stations conveniently located throughout Seoul, including near Hangang,** so you can plan your adventure with ease. Don't miss out on the excitement and beauty of the Hangang bike trails!

Price:
1 Hour – 1,000 Won
2 Hours – 2,000 Won
1 Day – 5,000 Won

Every 5 minutes thereafter you will be charged ₩200.

After locating an available bike, you can easily purchase a pass through the website or app and receive a number code to unlock the bike, allowing you to explore the city at your leisure. Returning the bike is easy, as you can drop it off at any Seoul Bike station.

ROYAL PALACES OF SEOUL
Discover the Gems of Korean History

The five royal palaces of Seoul boast stunning architecture, immaculate gardens, and fascinating historical significance that will transport you back in time to give you a glimpse into Korea's rich and fascinating history. Plus, enjoy fun cultural activities such as wearing traditional hanbok clothing, and watching traditional performances.

The best route to visit all five palaces in one day would be to start with **Gyeongbokgung** in the morning and work your way east to **Changdeokgung** and **Changgyeonggung**. From there, you can head south to **Deoksugung** and end your day at **Gyeonghuigung** in the western part of the city. Take the subway to save time and avoid traffic.

1 Gyeongbokgung 경복궁

Jongno-gu, Sajik-ro 161 종로구 사직로 161
3 min walk (0.14 miles / 225 m) from
Gyeongbokgung Station Exit #5 Subway Line 3

2 Changdeokgung 창덕궁

Jongno-gu, Yulgok-ro 99 종로구 율곡로 99
6 min walk (0.24 miles / 381 m)
from **Anguk Station Exit #3 Subway Line 3**

3 Changgyeonggung 창경궁

Jongno-gu, Changgyeonggung-ro 185 종로구 창경궁로 185
13 min walk (0.48 miles / 771 m) from
Hyehwa Station Exit #4 Subway Line 4

4 Deoksugung 덕수궁

Jung-gu, Sejong-daero 99 중구 세종대로 99
1 min walk (0.05 miles / 80 m) from **City Hall Station Exit #2 Subway Line 1**

5 Gyeonghuigung 경희궁

Jongno-gu, Saemunan-ro 45 종로구 새문안로 45
10 min walk (0.40 miles / 639 m) from
Seodaemun Station Exit #4 Subway Line 5

6 Cheong Wa Dae 청와대

Jongno-gu Cheongwadae-ro 1 종로구 청와대로 1
24 min walk (0.86 miles / 1.4 km) from
Gyeongbokgung Station Exit #3 Subway Line 3

This is **not** a royal palace but a **residence** that served for **previous Korean presidents**. Recently, it has been opened to the general public. We highly recommend visiting this stunning location as part of your tour!

1 GYEONGBOKGUNG 경복궁
"Palace Greatly Blessed by Heaven"

Gyeonghokgung is located in the northern part of Seoul and is **the largest** of the five palaces. It was the main palace during the Joseon Dynasty and features numerous **pavilions**, **gardens**, and **courtyards**.

Jan - Feb: 9 a.m. - 5 p.m.
Mar -May: 9 a.m. - 6 p.m.
Jun - Aug: 9 a.m. - 6:30 p.m.
Sep - Oct: 9 a.m. - 6 p.m.
Nov - Dec: 9 a.m. - 5 p.m.
(last admission is 1 hour before closing.)

*Closed on **Tuesday** (if a national holiday falls on a Tuesday, it's closed the following day.)
*Offers **Seasonal Night Tour Program**. Check website for most up-to-date hours.

Age 19~64 3,000 won / 2.400 won (group, 10 or more)
- Free: Ages 18 and under, Ages 65 and above / For wearing Hanbok
- Get a **Combination Ticket/Royal Palace Pass** 통합관람권 for 10,000 won (vs. 14,000 won separately) to access **Gyeongbokgung**, **Changdeokgung** (with Secret Garden), **Changgyeonggung**, **Deoksugung**, and **Jongmyo Shrine**. Valid for three months. Purchase on-site at the time of visit.
  *It does *not* include **Gyeonghuigung**.

SCAN FOR MAP!

SCAN FOR DIRECTIONS!

WHAT'S AROUND THE PALACE?

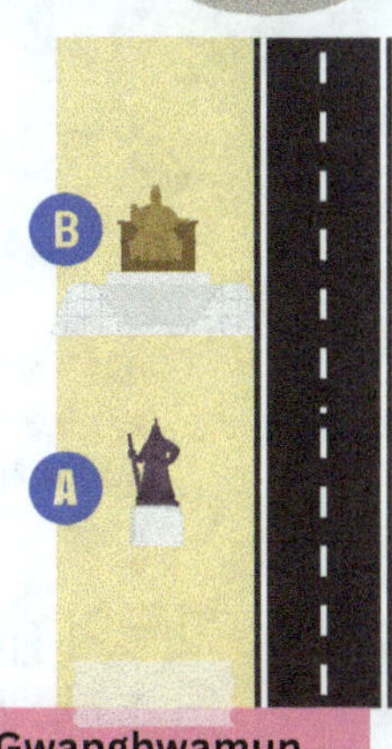

Gwanghwamun Square

A Statue of Admiral Yi Sun-Sin

Take an Epic Photo with a Legendary Korean War Hero!

The statue commemorates **Admiral Yi Sun-sin** 이순신 a legendary naval commander of the **Joseon Dynasty**, celebrated for his strategic brilliance and the victories against Japanese invasions during the Imjin War in the late 16th century. The statue depicts Admiral Yi in his military attire, holding a sword, and gazing confidently towards the horizon. It serves as a symbol of courage, patriotism, and the indomitable spirit of the Korean people!

Can You Find the Legendary Turtle Ship?

Look closely at the bottom of the statue, and you'll find a **model of the armored Turtle Ship**, which was invented by Admiral Yi Sun-sin and played a crucial role in defeating the Japanese army. Keep an eye out for it!

Pose with the King and Snap a Photo!

The statue of **King Sejong the Great** commemorates his reign during the Joseon Dynasty. King Sejong is famous for his promotion of science, literature, and education. The statue shows him seated on a throne, holding a book, symbolizing his contributions to Korean culture and the **creation of Hangul, the Korean alphabet**. It stands as a reminder of his lasting legacy and serves as a symbol of Korean history and national pride.

Discover the Brilliant Inventions During King Sejong's Reign!

In front of the King's statue, you can find replicas of an **armillary sphere**, the world's first **rain gauge**, and a **sundial**, symbolizing the advanced science during the King's reign.

Visit the Secret Underground Museum!

Did you know that there's a hidden secret space behind the statue that even many Koreans aren't familiar with? It's actually an **underground museum** dedicated to **King Sejong** and **Admiral Yi Sun-sin**. Inside this expansive area, which is divided into two sections, you can delve into the lives and accomplishments of these two historical figures. The museum offers a wide range of **multimedia content** and **hands-on activities**, allowing visitors to have a firsthand experience. If you mention that you've visited this place, people will be genuinely amazed because it's quite a remarkable find!

Admission: Free
Hours: 10 a.m. to 6:30 p.m. (last admission 6 p.m.)
*Closed every Monday.

(If a legal holiday falls on a Monday, the museum will be open and instead closed on the following weekday.)

Make Various Souvenirs!

Visit a kiosk and unleash your creativity and design a one-of-a-kind badge, keychain, or pop socket by combining Korean elements with the iconic figures of King Sejong and Admiral Yi Sun-sin! **2,000 KRW (Card Only) 11 a.m. - 6 p.m.**

Learn to Write Your Name in Korean!

Learn to use a writing brush and write your name in Hangul! **Next to the King Sejong education center FREE 11 a.m. ~ 6 p.m.**

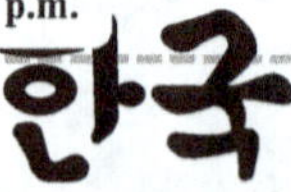

Gwanghwamun is the **biggest gate** of **Gyeongbokgung**, and it's called the "spreading light" gate. It was first built in 1395 and was an important landmark in Seoul when it was the capital during the Joseon Dynasty. Sadly, the gate has been damaged and ignored at different times. In 1592, during the Japanese invasion, it was burned down and left in ruins for over 250 years. But it went through numerous restoration projects and the most recent version was oepend to the public in 2010.

Choose Your Path Through Rainbow Gates!

Gwanghwamun has **three rainbow-shaped gates**, where history tells that the **king** used the **middle door**, **military officials** entered through the **left**, and **civil officials** through the **right**. Choose your favorite gate and step into a place of your choice!

Discover the Rising Phoenix Beneath the Arch!

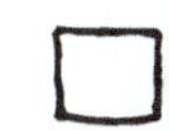

The Rising Phoenix is portrayed on the ceiling of the middle gate of Gwanghwamun, representing **one of the four guardians** responsible for defending the east, west, north, and south. It symbolizes the south direction. Let's enter the palace with the guidance of the Rising Phoenix!

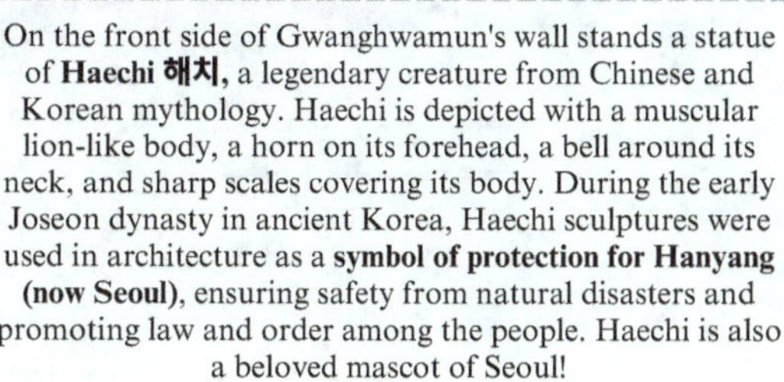

Take a Picture with the Statue of Haechi!

On the front side of Gwanghwamun's wall stands a statue of **Haechi 해치,** a legendary creature from Chinese and Korean mythology. Haechi is depicted with a muscular lion-like body, a horn on its forehead, a bell around its neck, and sharp scales covering its body. During the early Joseon dynasty in ancient Korea, Haechi sculptures were used in architecture as a **symbol of protection for Hanyang (now Seoul)**, ensuring safety from natural disasters and promoting law and order among the people. Haechi is also a beloved mascot of Seoul!

Rent a Hanbok and Get Free Admission!

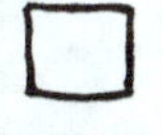

Immerse yourself in the palace life by donning an exquisite, full set of **Hanbok**. And here's the bonus: by wearing a complete Hanbok ensemble, **you can enjoy free admission to the palaces**. Please note that a T-shirt and Hanbok pants won't qualify as a full set.

Several Hanbok rental shops are conveniently located near **Gyeongbokgung Station Exit #4 on Subway Line 3.**

D National Palace Museum of Korea

gogung.go.kr

Explore Joseon Heritage Through Artifacts!

Situated **within Gyeongbokgung**, this museum showcases and oversees the **cultural treasures and historical items of the Joseon royal family**. It comprises two floors above the ground and one basement level, featuring a total of 15 exhibition spaces, presenting the history of the Joseon royal family, including various palaces, the Korean Empire, royal paintings, and rituals.

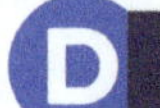

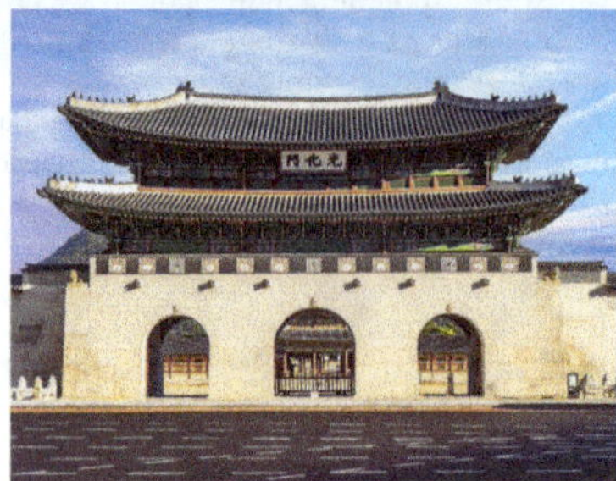

국립고궁박물관
Jongno-gu Hyoja-ro 12 종로구 효자로 12

EVERYDAY 9 a.m. - 6 p.m.
(last admission is 1 hour before closing.)
Closed on 1/1, Seollal, Chuseok

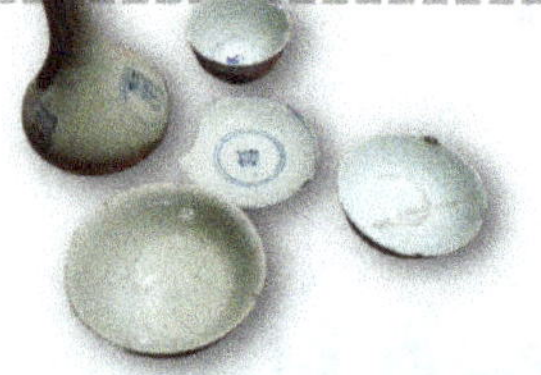

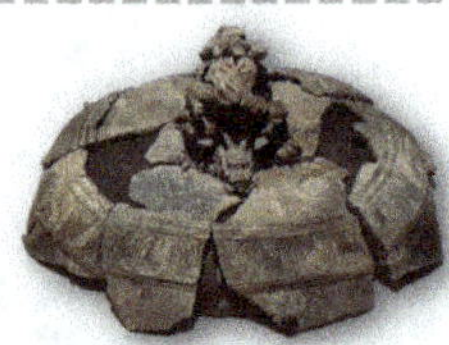

GEUNJEONGJEON 근정전 (MAIN HALL)

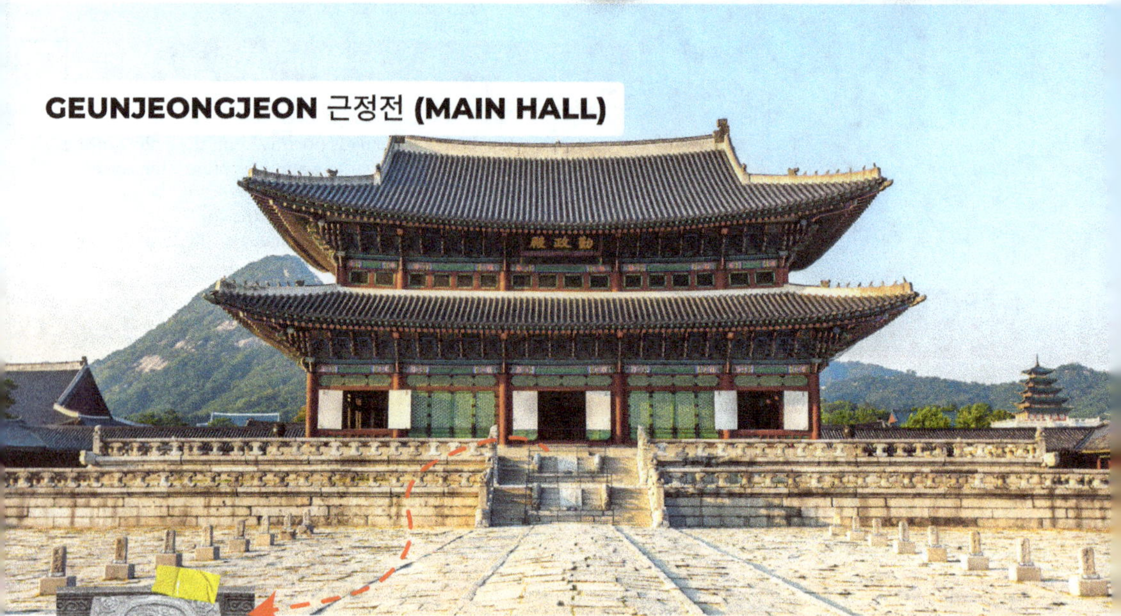

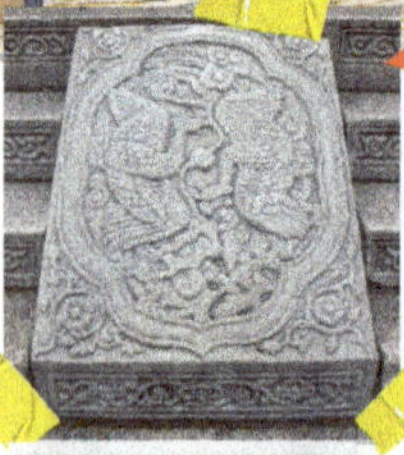

Spot the Legendary Phoenix Carved Into Stone!

Once you enter the palace, you'll come across a path that is divided into three sections, known as ***samdo* 삼도** or "three paths." The central path, which is the widest and highest, is called the royal path (***eodo* 어도**) and was exclusively used by the kings. The east path was for civil officials, while the west path was for military officials. In the palace complex, a **phoenix-shaped stone carving** is found along the king's path, symbolizing **peace and prosperity**. According to tradition, the king's palanquin would pass over this spot as he wouldn't walk directly on the ground.

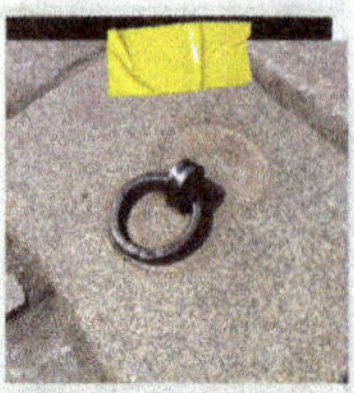

Find the Iron Loops Used to Set Up Tents!

On the court floor, you can find **iron loops made to set up tents** during important court events. These loops help keep out rain and sunlight. They were used to secure tents by tying a thick string to the iron loop, covering the sun when needed.

HYANGWONJEONG 향원정 PAVILION

Hyangwonjeong 향원정 is a small, two-story pavilion that was built in 1873 by King Gojong. It is shaped like a hexagon and is located on an artificial island called **Hyangwonji 향원지**. There is a bridge called **Chwihyanggyo 취향교**that connects the pavilion to the palace grounds. Hyangwonjeong means "pavilion of far-reaching fragrance" and Chwihyanggyo means "bridge intoxicated with fragrance." The original Chwihyanggyo was the longest wooden bridge during the Joseon Dynasty, but it was destroyed in the Korean War. It was later rebuilt in a different location in 1953, but now it is being moved back to its original place on the north side of the island.

Discover the Storage for Korean Fermented Foods!

Adjacent to Hyangwonjeong is *janggo* (**장고**), a **designated storage are**a for a wide range of pastes utilized in royal banquets, rituals, and meals. Here, you'll find an extensive collection of specialized earthenware vessels used for fermenting and preserving various food items such as *kimchi*, bean paste, and *gochujang*. These storage spaces were overseen by a court lady known as *janggo mama* **장고마마**.

Spot the Mysterious Mini Statues on the Roof!

GYEONGHOERU 경회루 (PAVILLION)

Gyeonghoeru 경회루 pavilion has all 11 statues on the roof!

When you look at the roofs of Korean palaces, you'll see mysterious statues called *japsang (***잡상**). These statues are placed in groups of odd numbers, usually up to 11. They come from an old Korean belief system and are meant to **keep away bad spirits and bad luck**, like how gargoyles do in Western stories. They also show that the buildings are important and impressive. This tradition might have come from China a long time ago, during the Joseon Dynasty, as the statues are believed to represent characters and gods from the Chinese classic literature, *Journey to the West*.

Discover the Wall of Longevity and Make a Wish for a Long Life!

Outside of **Jagyeongjeon (자경전)**, you will encounter *shipjangsaeng* (**십장생**), also known as the "Ten Symbols of Longevity." This traditional Korean pattern includes representations of the **sun, mountain, rock, water, cloud, pine tree, elixir plant, turtle, crane, and deer**. Each symbol holds significance for longevity, and when combined, they enhance their individual meanings.

Find Them All!

- ○ Sun
- ○ Mountain
- ○ Rock
- ○ Water
- ○ Cloud
- ○ Pine Tree
- ○ Elixir Plant
- ○ Turtle
- ○ Crane
- ○ Deer

Have Lunch Like Ancient Koreans Did!

Located near **Gyeongbokgung Station**, **Tongin Market** is a **lively dining spot** on the **second floor** that offers a unique lunch experience. Here, you can purchase your meal using *Yupjeon* **엽전**, traditional coins from the Joseon Dynasty. Once you exchange your money for these special coins, you can select your own **customized lunch box**.

풍이엉니 blog.naver.com/jjeung2_(CC BY 2.0 KR)

Take a Journey Tracing Ordinary Korean Life

E National Folk Museum of Korea

nfm.go.kr

This museum was built in 1946 and merged with the National Museum of Korea, and 4,555 artifacts were moved to Mt. Namsan. In 1993, it opened at its current place **inside Gyeongbokgung**. The museum has **over 98,000 artifacts** that vividly show the **history of everyday life for regular Korean people**. It's a great place to compare the lives of kings and ordinary people in Korea's history. Plus, there are lots of fun **activities for everyone to enjoy!**

국립민속박물관
Jongno-gu, Samcheong-ro 37 종로구 삼청로 37

EVERYDAY 9 a.m. - 6 p.m.
(last admission is 1 hour before closing.)
Closed on 1/1, Seollal, Chuseok

② CHANGDEOKGUNG 창덕궁
"Palace of Prospering Virtue"

Cheangdeokgung is located in the eastern part of Seoul and is known for its **beautiful gardens and natural landscapes**. It was the favored palace of many Joseon Dynasty kings and is a **UNESCO World Heritage** site.

Feb - May: 9 a.m. - 6 p.m.
Jun - Aug: 9 a.m. - 6:30 p.m.
Sep - Oct: 9 a.m. - 6 p.m.
Nov - Jan: 9 a.m. - 5:30 p.m.
(Last admission 1 hour before closing)

*Closed on **Monday** (if a national holiday falls on a Monday, it's closed the following day)
Offers **Seasonal Night Tour Program. Check website for most up-to-date hours.

Age 19~64 1,000 won / 800 won (group, 10 or more)
- Free: Ages 18 and under, Ages 65 and above / For wearing Hanbok
- Huwon 후원 (Secret Garden) has a limit of 100 people per session (50 online / 50 on-site reservation)
  It's strongly recommended that you make a reservation online in advance

SCAN FOR DIRECTIONS!

Locate the Scary Korean Goblin On the Stone Bridge!

Every Korean royal palace had a stream running through it, and there was a stone bridge over the stream. They made statues of goblins, called *dokkaebi* 도깨비, and carved them into the stone bridges. People believed that these goblin statues and other scary creatures would **keep away evil spirits and keep the palace safe**.

GEUMCHEONGYO 금천교

karendotcom127 flickr.com/photos/karendotcom127 (CC BY 2.0)

Explore Injeongjeon Hall's Modern Transformation!

Injeongjeon Hall, which became a **gateway to foreign cultures** during the late Joseon Dynasty's diplomatic relations, underwent modernization with Western additions like windows, light bulbs, and curtains. This transition continued when King Sunjong moved to Changdeokgung Palace in 1907, leading to the replacement of the traditional *jeondol* 전돌 (brick) flooring with modern flooring and the introduction of electric light bulbs.

INJEONGJEON HALL 인정전

Spot the Traditional Korean Fire Extinguisher!

In the corners of the halls, there are special **bronze jars** called *deumeu* 드므 or *deumu* 드무. They're filled with water to **stop fires and keep away bad fire spirits**. People thought these spirits would see themselves in the water and get scared. In winter, they put fires nearby to keep the water from freezing. This shows how they combined their beliefs and scientific reasoning!

Find the Door That is a Tribute to the Full Moon's Beauty!

NAKSEONJAE 낙선재

Constructed in 1847, **Nakseonjae 낙선재** was established as a **retreat and study area for King Heonjong**. Renowned as the final residence of the royal family, its interior boasts a circular door **resembling a full moon**, showcasing the Joseon Dynasty's artistic sensibility.

Dadreot. via wikimedia commons CC BY-SA 3.0

느꽃지기 blog.naver.com/kwwoolim (CC BY 2.0 KR)

In the back of the residence lies a **lovely garden**, next to a modest and graceful pavilion named **Sangryangjeong 상량정**. On the western fence, you can also find a **circular entrance made of bricks**. It stands as the last remaining palace gate with this distinctive round shape. Inside, it contains **sliding doors that move from side to side**.

Discover the Palace's Secret Garden!

Originally constructed during the Joseon Dynasty, the **Secret Garden (Huwon 후원)** served as a **private retreat for the royal family**, offering them a peaceful escape from the demands of court life. Today, visitors can embark on guided tours to explore its serene landscapes, meandering pathways, beautiful ponds, and traditional pavilions.

Entrance is separate from the main palace, requiring a separate ticket for the tour. Due to its delicate nature, daily visitor numbers are limited, and entry is granted through timed tours. Check the website for more info.

HUWON 후원

Find the Outdoor Bar Used for a Fun Drinking Session!

In the Huwon ("Rear Garden") area, there's a stream called **Ongnyucheon 옥류천** ("Jade Stream"). It has a **U-shaped water channel** made in 1636 for **floating wine cups**. There's also a small **waterfall** and a **poem** written on **a big rock** above it. Additionally, you can find **five small pavilions** in that area.

3 CHANGGYEONGGUNG 창경궁
"Palace of Magnificent Joy"

Changgyeonggung is located in the eastern part of Seoul, next to Changdeokgung. It was originally built as a **summer palace** but was later converted to a **botanical garden**.
*You may start from Changdeokgung Palace and come through the Rear Garden 후원 (Huwon).

Everday 9 a.m. - 9 p.m.
(Last admission 1 hour before closing)

*Closed on **Monday**
(If a national holiday falls on a Monday, it's closed the following day)
*Offers **Seasonal Night Tour Program.** Check website for most up-to-date hours.

Age 19~64 1,000 won / 800 won (group, 10 or more)
- Free: Ages 18 and under, Ages 65 and above / For wearing Hanbok

Experience a Day in the Life of a Court Official!

MYEONGJEONJEON 명정전 (MAIN HALL)

"Rank stones," known as *pumgyeseok* 품계석, are neatly arranged in two rows, offering insight into the world of **court officials and their roles** during ceremonies. Choose your preferred rank and stand beside it to capture a photo!

Discover the Royal Throne of the King with Majestic Phoenixes Soaring Overhead!

Wei-Te Wong flickr.com/photos/wongwt (CC BY-SA 2.0)

The **Phoenix Throne**, or **eojwa 어좌** symbolizes the king's ultimate authority, carrying a profound significance. The phoenix holds a longstanding connection with **Korean royalty**, evident in various aspects such as the tomb murals of the Goguryeo Kingdom 고구려.

Irworobongdo 일월오봉도, also recognized as the "**Sun, Moon, and Five Peaks Painting**," is a traditional Korean folding screen displayed **behind the royal throne** in the Joseon Dynasty. It portrays a stylized landscape with the sun, moon, and five peaks, symbolizing the king, the queen, and a mythical land. This screen splendidly showcased the majesty of the Joseon royal court.

Discover the Sacred Royal Placenta Chamber!

Taesil 태실, meaning "placenta chamber," is a structure built to enshrine the **umbilical cord** and **placenta** of **King Seongjong** 선종, who reigned from 1469 to 1494. This practice was rooted in the tradition and belief of the Dynasty, which held that preserving the placentas of royal heirs at auspicious sites throughout the country was linked to the destiny of the ruling family.

Tell Which Way the Wind Is Blowing with This Stone Instrument!

Wei-Te Wong flickr.com/photos/wongwt *(CC BY-SA 2.0)*

Punggidae 풍기대 is a **stone measuring device** used to determine **wind speed and direction**. A pole is inserted into a hole at the top of the stone, with a piece of cloth attached to the end of the pole to indicate the movement of the wind.

Find the Sundial and Try to Tell Time!

Angbuilgu 앙부일구 is a **sundial shaped like an upturned cauldron**, created during the reign of King Sejong in 1434 and is renowned for its ability to display the local solar time and the twenty-four solar terms.

*This is a replica, and the actual artifact is kept in the **National Palace Museum** located inside Gyeongbokgung.*

Discover Diverse Plants in Korea's first Western-Style Greenhouse!

Established in 1909, **Daeonsil** 대온실 (**"Grand Greenhouse"**) is Korea's **first western-style greenhouse**, constructed alongside a palace zoo by the Japanese colonial government. Designed by a Japanese architect and constructed by a French firm, the structure fuses steel and wood, with a glass exterior. It initially showcased exotic plants and later transitioned to featuring indigenous Korean plants after the palace's restoration in 1986.

DEOKSUGUNG 덕수궁
"Palace of Virtuous Longevity"

Deoksugung is located in the heart of Seoul, near City Hall. It was the **residence of the royal family** during the late Joseon Dynasty and features a **mix of traditional and modern (Western) architecture.**

Everday 9 a.m. - 9 p.m.
(Last admission 1 hour before closing)

*Closed on **Monday**
(If a national holiday falls on a Monday, it's closed the following day)
*Offers **Seasonal Night Tour Program.** Check website for most up-to-date hours.

Age 19~64 1,000 won / 800 won (group, 10 or more)
- Free: Ages 18 and under, Ages 65 and above / For wearing Hanbok

SCAN FOR DIRECTIONS!

SCAN FOR MAP!

Watch the Authentic Royal Guard Changing Ceremony!

This is **Daehanmun** 대한문, which is also the ticket booth for the palace.

In the Joseon Dynasty, the **Royal Guard** was like a **national defense** and helped the **king keep control and order**. It started with the first gate guard in 1469 when King Yejong became the king. Later, rules for managing gate guards were added to the National Code during the reign of King Seongjong. In 1906, a ceremony to change the royal guard in front of the Daehanmun Gate began, making it the main entrance to the Palace.

The ceremony is held every day at 11 a.m. and 2 p.m. (Except Monday)

Check Out the Amazing Artwork on the Dragon Drum!

The **yonggo** 용고, also called the "**dragon drum**," is a barrel drum used in **military music** called *daechwita* 대취타. It has tacked heads with painted dragon designs. It's struck with two padded sticks.

Beyond the Gate lies **Geumcheongyo** 금천교 (has the same name as the one at Changdeokgung, constructed in 1411 and later excavated and restored in 1986. It is the oldest surviving bridge in Seoul. Upon entering the gate, you will traverse a stream, which represents a sacred pool found in every royal palace. This act signifies **purifying oneself before entering**.

Spot the Soaring Phoenix and Dragon on the Roof Tiles!

The tile pattern on **Yuhyeonmun 유현문**, which leads to **Hamnyeongjeon 함녕전**, the king's bedroom, showcases the vibrant designs of **phoenix** and **dragon**. These patterns symbolize the **king's authority**.

Find the Mystic Symbols on the Western-Style Architect!

Located on the hill of the rear garden, overlooking the palace, **Jeonggwanheon 정관헌** is a building constructed around 1900 for **relaxation** and **entertainment**. It incorporates both **Korean and Western architectural elements** and was designed by a Russian architect. The upper columns of the building are adorned with carvings featuring traditional Korean motifs, including blue and gold **dragons**, **bats**, and **flower vases**.

Bats have been regarded as symbols of **good luck**, warding off **evil spirits** and symbolizing **fertility**.

The symbol of a deer carrying an **herb of eternal youth**, known as *bulocho* 불로초.

The Western-style tiles on the floor of Jeonggwanheon.

Seokjojeon 석조전 is a historic building constructed in 1900 as the **main hall** and **residence** of King Gojong. Designed by a British architect, it combines Western and Korean architectural styles and it had witnessed significant events and was restored in the 1990s. **From the lawn across the water fountain,** you can capture a **photo that beautifully merges the past and present of Korea,** blending Western influences with Korean traditions!

Seokjojeon comprises of the **Donggwan 동관** (East Building) and **Seogwan 서관** (West Building). The main building, **Donggwan,** is currently home to the **Daehan (Korean) Empire History Museum,** displaying artifacts related to the royal family, while the **Seogwan,** added later, now houses the **National Museum of Modern and Contemporary Art.**

Daehan Empire History Museum (Donggwan) Tue - Sun : 9:30 a.m. - 4:30 p.m. **Closed Mon**

You can freely explore the Ground Floor without a reservation. 1st and 2nd floor requires a reservation.

deoksugung.go.kr

National Museum of Modern and Contemporary Art (Seogwan)
Tue, Thur, Fri, Sun : 10 a.m. - 6 p.m. / Wed, Sat : 10 a.m. - 9 p.m. / **Mon Closed**

mmca.go.kr

You can visit the Ground Floor.

There is a particular location in Seoul that you might want to avoid exploring with your significant other - the **Deoksugung Doldamgil 덕수궁 돌담길,** also known as the "**stonewall path.**" This path runs alongside the stone wall surrounding the Deoksugung area appears delightful at first glance.

However, there exists an **urban legend** suggesting that walking along this trail can lead to the **break up of couples.** While the exact origins of this belief remain unclear, it is worth noting that the path eventually leads to the **Seoul Family Court,** where many couples seeking separation have to pass through. Dare to test your luck?

In close proximity to Deoksugung Palace, there is a **unique Starbucks store** that can only be found in Korea. The **Hwangudan 환구단** store is exquisitely designed with **traditional Korean Hanok architecture,** serving as inspiration for its interior decor and items.

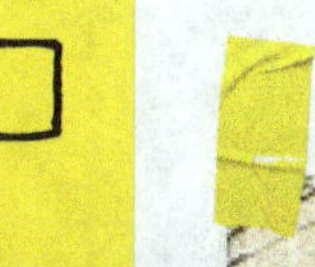

Starbucks Hwangudan
스타벅스 환구단점
Jung-gu Sogong-ro 112
중구 소공로 112

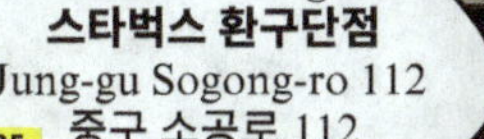

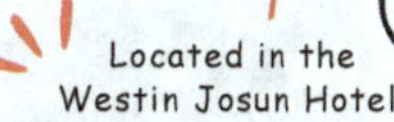

Located in the Westin Josun Hotel!

5 GYEONGHUIGUNG 경희궁
"Palace of Joy and Harmony"

The Palace's construction concluded in 1620. After the Japanese invasion in 1592, it became a detached palace, known as the **West Palace**, separate from the royal residence, **Changdeokgung**. In its prime, Gyeonghuigung housed **over 100 halls**; however, fires destroyed most, and the remaining ones were dismantled to expand Gyeongbokgung. After the 1945 liberation, **Seoul High School** was established here until 1978. In 1985, **restoration work**, including Sungjeongjeon Hall, was undertaken.

Everday 9 a.m. - 6 p.m.
(Last admission 1 hour before closing)

*Closed on **Monday**
(If a national holiday falls on a Monday, it's closed the following day)

Free Admission

Take a Peek into the Life of the King!

Within the **Sungjeongjeon 숭정전** lies a captivating **mini exhibition** that vividly **reenacts life within the palace**. Immerse yourself in the experience of sitting upon the Phoenix Throne and relive the splendor of this meticulously restored space, gaining a glimpse into what it must have felt like in the past.

SUNGJEONGJEON 숭정전

Use the picture to help you locate and identify all **17 royal items inside the building**. Try to guess what each item was used for based on its appearance and context!

Can You Spot All 17 Royal Items?

1. Royal Screen
2. Honor Flag (Cheongseon 청선)
3. Incense Support / Vase
4. Royal Throne
5. Secretary's Seat
6. Reading Table
7. Inkstone Table
8. Historiographer's Seat
9. Lamp
10. Honor Flag (Parasol 일산)
11. Honor Flag (Dragon Fan 용선)
12. Honor Flag (Phoenix Fan 봉선)
13. Sword
14. Honor Flag (Hongyangsan 홍양산)
15. Honor Flag (Geumwolbu 금월부)
16. Honor Flag (Sujeongjang 수정장)
17. Incense Burner / Incense

TAERYEONGJEON 태령전

Meet the Portrait of King Yeongjo!

Initially, **Taeryeongjeon 태령전** had no specific purpose or function. However, in 1744, during the 20th year of King Yeongjo's reign, a renovation took place, and a special spot was designated for the **king's portrait** within the structure.

Discover the Reason the Palace Was Built - the King's Rock!

Originally known as **Wangam 왕암 (King's Rock)**, **Seoam 서암** is the name given to the rock situated behind Taeryeongjeon. The name "Wangam" came about due to a popular belief that Gwanghaegun, a former king, sensed a **regal energy** emanating from the rock and chose to establish Gyeonghuigung in its vicinity. In 1708, during the 34th year of King Sukjong's reign, it was officially renamed as Seoam, and King Sukjong himself personally wrote the name in Chinese characters, which were then grandly engraved on a stone.

WITHIN THE PALACE SITE

Seoul Museum of History

museum.seoul.go.kr

Embark on a Time Travel to Explore Seoul's Past and Present!

The museum offers a comprehensive journey through **Seoul's history and culture**, spanning from prehistoric eras to the modern age. From the illustrious Joseon Dynasty to the period of Japanese colonial rule, you can immerse yourself in the remarkable evolution of Seoul, particularly its remarkable advancements following the Korean War.

Jjw, (CC BY-SA 3.0), via Wikimedia Commons

서울역사박물관
Jongno-gu Saemunan-ro 55 종로구 새문안로 5

EVERYDAY 9 a.m. - 6 p.m.
(last admission 5:30 p.m.)
Closed on Monday and 1/1)

6 CHEONG WA DAE 청와대
"The Former Residence of Korean Presidents"

Also known as the "Blue House" due to its unique blue tiles, this building **was constructed in 1946 and functioned as the South Korean president's office and residence until 2022**. Now open to the public, the establishment spans about 62 acres and was built within the historical grounds of the Joseon Dynasty's royal garden. Its stunning location near Bugaksan Mountain offers an incredible experience for visitors in Korea. To learn about **available programs and register, make sure to visit the website.**

SCAN FOR DIRECTIONS!

자부 blog.naver.com/zaab
(CC BY 2.0 KR)

Mar - Nov 9 a.m. - 6 p.m. (Last admission 5:30 p.m.)
Dec - Feb 9 a.m. - 5:30 p.m. (Last admission 5 p.m.)
(By **reservation** and **on-site applications**)

Free Admission

*Closed on **Tuesday**
(If a national holiday falls on a Tuesday, it's closed the following day)

On-site application details:
- Eligibility: Senior citizens aged 65 or older, persons with disabilities (can have 1 additional person), those eligible for national veterans benefits, and foreigners
- Application locations: **Main Gate Information Center** or **Chunchumun 춘추문 Information Center**

Maximum number of participants
Individual reservation: 6
Group reservation: 20-50
65 or over/Disabled applicants: 6

> opencheongwadae.kr/eng
>
> *The reservation page is presented only in Korean. You might have to use your browser's translation feature.*

> *You can enter and exit from either point, and there is no time limit for your viewing experience.*

Take an Autonomous Bus to Get There!

> Blend of heritage and cutting-edge! Experience a ride on our autonomous bus. This innovative bus shuttles along the Gyeongbokgung Stonewall Walk, covering a 1.6 mi / 2.6 km route. No reservation needed –
> just hop on and enjoy the journey!

Bus #A01
Bus stop : near the Main Entrance of the **National Palace Museum of Korea (Gyeongbokgung) / Next to Exit #5 Gyeongbokgung Station Subway Line 3**

Hours :
(Mon–Fri) 9 a.m. –5 p.m.
(12 p.m. - 1 p.m. break);
(Sat–Sun) 9:30 a.m. –5 p.m.
(12 p.m. - 1 p.m. break)

Fare :
Free (transportation card required)

SCAN FOR DIRECTIONS!

Sarangchae 사랑채 (located right across the Cheongwadae Bus Stop) is a place where visitors can learn about Cheong Wa Dae's history and what it does. Inside, you'll find a chair set up like the president's chair. Sit in it and imagine being the president of South Korea!

Walk under this Gate for Eternal Youth!

Don't forget to step beneath the charming **Bulomun 불로문 gate** at the entrance of the **Small Garden**. Legend has it that passing under brings eternal youth. So, go ahead and make your wish for a life filled with health and longevity – the garden invites you to embrace this hopeful tradition.

자부 blog.naver.com/zaaboo (CC BY 2.0 KR)

Step into the Role of a Presidential Spokesperson!

Chunchugwan 춘추관 acts as a press center for Cheong Wa Dae, providing updates to the media about policies and important matters. Why not stand tall and capture a memorable photo here? If stress doesn't faze you, perhaps being a presidential spokesperson could be your calling!

쬬리 blog.naver.com/jj0ry (CC BY-SA 2.0 KR)

Take the Heritage Trail to Enjoy the View from High Up!

자부 blog.naver.com/zaaboo (CC BY 2.0 KR)

Surrounded by beautiful nature, the Heritage Trail provides amazing views of Cheong Wa Dae and Seoul from the Bugaksan Mountain. You can start by taking the path behind the presidential residence. The uphill hike is about 1673 ft. / 510 meters and gives you wide views of places like Gyeongbok and modern Seoul. You'll also see the peaceful Ounjeong Pavilion and find an ancient Stone Seated Buddha. This trail mixes history, nature, and modern life, making it a 30-minute adventure you'll always remember. Once you finish, you'll be back at the main office building.

Hanok Villages

Step Back in Time and Experience Korean Lifestyle

Experience the **unique beauty of traditional Korean architecture** as you wander through the streets of these historic neighborhoods. Immerse yourself in the traditional Korean way of life and gain a deeper understanding of the country's rich culture and heritage. These villages offer a glimpse into Korea's past with their **charming cafes**, **local shops**, and **stunning architectural details**.

SCAN FOR DIRECTIONS!

Bukchon Hanok Village 북촌 한옥마을 Jongno-gu, Gahoe-dong 31-48 종로구 가회동 31-48
17 min walk (0.53 miles / 865 m) from **Anguk Station Exit #2 Subway Line 3**

Situated **between Gyeongbokgung and Changdeokgung** in the heart of Seoul, it stands out as a spacious and extensive location. It boasts approximately **900 well-preserved traditional Hanok houses** that are still occupied by local residents. While primarily functioning as a residential area, some houses have been transformed into **cultural centers**, **guesthouses**, and **shops**, providing visitors with insights into the **daily lives of the residents**. Moreover, the village is nestled between two palaces, offering **breathtaking views of traditional architecture** juxtaposed against Seoul's **modern skyline**.

Capture the Perfect Selfie at the Most Scenic Photo Spot!

Bukchon Hanok Village is a popular destination among foreign tourists, and it frequently serves as a **backdrop in dramas and movies**. One particular area that stands out is the photo spot located atop the tile-roofed houses. It's truly a sight to behold!

It's approximately a 15-minute walk from **Anguk Station**.

Indulge in the Renowned Hand-torn Noodle Dish!

Samcheongdong Sujebi 삼청동 수제비
Jongno-gu, Samcheong-ro 101-1
종로구 삼청로 101-1
Everyday 11 a.m. - 9 p.m.

Established in 1982 and recently **Michelin Guide-recognized**, this beloved restaurant is renowned for its delicate *sujebi* 수제비 **(hand-torn) noodles** in flavorful anchovy broth, they also offer delightful **all-potato potato pancakes**.

💡 Visiting outside of lunchtime can lead to quicker entry.

Savor the Beautiful Surroundings with a Sip of Korean Tea!

Cha Teul 차마시는 뜰
Jongno-gu, Bukchon-ro 11na-gil 26 종로구 북촌로11나길 26

Sun : 11 a.m. - 9 p.m.
Tue - Fri : 12 p.m. - 9 p.m.
Mon Closed

Nestled in a picturesque setting among **traditional Korean architecture and gardens**, this tea house provides an authentic encounter with **Korea's traditional tea culture**. With offerings including bellflower, plum, jujube, and silver grass teas, visitors can savor these with classic **Korean sweets and rice cakes**.

SCAN FOR DIRECTIONS!

구링빠 blog.naver.com/donggoo1214 (CC BY-SA 2.0 KR)

Visit the Filming Place of the Movie "The Assassination"!

This house is notable for its appearances in "**The Assassination**" and "**Reborn Rich**," holds historical value as the former residence of Baek In-je, the Baek Hospital founder. Being **Seoul's second-largest traditional house**, it offers free admission and a photo spot in the annex, inviting visitors to capture its essence through pictures.

Jongno-gu, Gahoe-dong 11-7
종로구 가회동 11-7
The House of Baek Inje 백인제 가옥
Tue - Sun : 9 a.m. - 6 p.m. Mon Closed

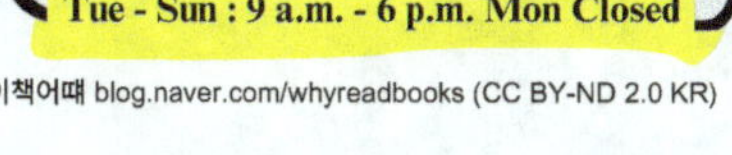

이책어때 blog.naver.com/whyreadbooks (CC BY-ND 2.0 KR)

Learn to Create a Traditional Korean Knot!

Explore the **elegance of traditional Korean ornamental knots** like tassels, waistbands, and fan ornaments, harmoniously presented with contemporary designs in this workshop. Appreciate the fusion of heritage and innovation, and join their hands-on class to craft a cell phone string, wristband, and necklace using the time-honored Korean knot technique. This dedicated **workshop** blends history and creativity while offering arts and crafts education for all expertise levels.

SCAN FOR DIRECTIONS!

Tue - Sun 10 a.m. – 6 p.m.   shimyoungmi.com

Participate in Bukchon's Diverse Craft Programs!

This space offers an **experience center**, an **education center**, and an **exhibition hall**, providing ample opportunities to **learn and engage with traditional Korean crafts**. Despite its small size, it offers a diverse range of craft programs that vary by the day of the week and are conducted in small groups of around 10 people. Anyone can participate in the traditional craft activities **without needing a reservation!**

SCAN FOR DIRECTIONS!

Mar - Oct : Everyday 10 a.m. – 6 p.m.
Nov - Feb 10 a.m. - 5 p.m. (Except Seollal & Chuseok)   Tel: 02-741-2148

Bless a Couple Having a Wedding!

Bukchon Hanok Village is not only a popular tourist destination but also a highly sought-after place for **weddings**. If you happen to be fortunate, you might come across a couple exchanging vows! How about sharing a heartfelt word of blessing for their special day?

Explore Korean Folk Art and Discover Your Artistic Talent!

With a dedicated focus on **folk paintings**, the museum's vast and captivating collection comprises **2,000 relics from the illustrious Joseon Dynasty**. Visitors are warmly welcomed to partake in a diverse range of **folk painting experiences**, from drawing talismans to coloring folk paintings, and even creating their own fans adorned with intricate folk-painting designs.

Tue - Sun : 10 am - 6 pm
gahoemuseum.org

SCAN FOR DIRECTIONS!

Namsangol Hanok Village 남산골 한옥 마을 Jung-gu, Toegye-ro 34-gil 28 중구 퇴계로34길 28
6 min walk (0.19 miles / 306 m) from **Chungmuro Station Exit #4 Subway Line 3 or 4**

hanokmaeul.or.kr Tue - Sun : 9 a.m. - 8 p.m. Mon Closed

SCAN FOR DIRECTIONS!

Namsangol Hanok Village rests at the **base of Namsan Mountain, close to Myeongdong**. It is a **smaller village** featuring **five traditional Hanok houses**, purposefully established as a **tourist destination**, offering the opportunity to **explore and reconnect with the lives of their ancestors**. One of its key advantages is that it allows visitors to experience the interiors and gain a deeper understanding of traditional Korean architecture and customs. You can partake in **cultural programs**, enjoy **performances**, and explore exhibitions.

Find a House Decorated with Traditional Korean Lanterns!

Capture a photo of a house adorned with *cheongsachorong* 청사초롱, a **traditional Korean lantern**. These lanterns are typically created by combining red and blue silk shades and placing a candle inside the body. While traditionally used in wedding ceremonies, they are now commonly showcased in various cultural exhibitions throughout Korea.

Learn about the Science Behind the Traditional Heating System, Ondol!

When you enter the kitchen of a Hanok house, you'll discover how Korean people kept their homes warm during the winter. The *agungi* 아궁이, a heating platform for the cauldron, utilized residual heat to warm the floors of the rooms. This heating system was known as *ondol* 온돌, and this is something you can experience at *jjimjilbang* 찜질방, a Korean spa.

Find a House With a Shrine for Ancestors!

Within traditional Korean houses, it was customary to establish **shrines dedicated to paying respects to ancestors**. Explore a house with such a shrine and see what offerings are placed on the table!

See a Traditional Korean Wedding Ceremony in Action!

If there's a wedding taking place, you are welcome to **observe the ceremony from outside**. It's a real wedding and not a reenactment!

**Mar — Nov
(excluding Jul and Aug)
Sat and Sun
11:00 / 13:00 / 15:00**

Korean Street Food Showdown

Enjoy Korea's Most Beloved Street Eats!

Indulge in the **authentic flavors of Korean street eateries** and immerse yourself in the vibrant atmosphere where locals gather to savor their favorite dishes. Experience the true essence of local dining, just **like a local resident**!

Gwangjang Market 광장시장

Jongno-gu, Changgyeonggung-ro 88
종로구 창경궁로 88

SCAN FOR DIRECTIONS!

5 min walk (0.18 miles / 296 m) from
Jongno-5(o)-ga Station Exit #8 Subway Line 1

Gwangjang Market is a **lively traditional market** that foreigners should visit for an **exciting cultural experience**. At the market, you can find a variety of things to see and taste, including delicious Korean **street food**, beautiful **textiles**, and **handmade crafts**.

Try the Local's Favorite "Kim Tteok Soon" Trio!

"Kim Tteok Soon 김떡순" is a playful abbreviation that represents the beloved Korean street foods trio: **Kim**bab 김밥, **Tteok**bokki 떡볶이, and **Soon**dae 순대. These dishes are so popular among locals, to the point it gets a name like a real person!

Kimbap 김밥 : Korean roll consisting of seasoned rice, various fillings such as vegetables, meat, and pickles.

Tteokbokki 떡볶이 : Chewy rice cakes cooked ingochujang (hot and sweet pepper paste), often served with fish cakes and vegetables.

Soondae 순대 : Korean sausage made from pig's blood, rice, and various seasonings.

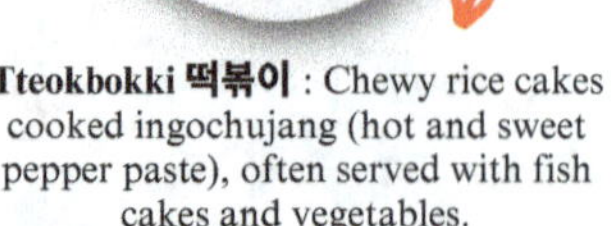

SCAN FOR DIRECTIONS!

Pojangmacha (포장마차), often shortened to "pocha," means "covered wagon". Originally, it was a **simple mobile outdoor restaurant** operating in **tented carts.** It used to be a popular choice for Koreans seeking a **quick and affordable meal** with a bottle of *soju* after work. However, with the emergence of establishments catering to younger patrons, it has recently transformed into a **charming spot for dates**. Pojangmachas also frequently appear as **backdrops in K-Dramas**.

Pop Open a Bottle of Soju the Korean Way!

Before opening a bottle of *soju*, shake it or swirl it fast to create a little tornado in the bottle.

Bang the bottom of the bottle with the elbow.

Twist open the screw cap and hit the neck of the bottle with a gentle Taekwondo chop, or make a V shape with your hand and hit the neck of the bottle between them, to get the top portion of the soju to splash out of the bottle.

In the past, *soju* bottles had corkscrews that could break and leave small pieces inside the bottle if not stored correctly. To get rid of these pieces, people started shaking and swirling the bottle. They would then bang the bottom to make the pieces come to the top, making it easier to remove them. Even though soju bottles now have screw caps and the ritual doesn't serve a practical purpose anymore, many still do it for fun.

Challenge Yourself to Try Dried Little Pollacks!

Make Yourself a Somaek Cocktail!

Somaek 소맥 (soju + **maekju** 맥주 "beer") is the number one choice among Koreans who lack the time but want to reap the benefits of alcohol in the shortest amount of time possible! The 3:7 ratio (soju:beer) is the most popular formula. Try one (only if you're over 19).

Despite their somewhat unappealing appearance, dried little pollacks, also known as *nogari* 노가리, are a popular accompaniment for drinking and offer numerous health benefits. (Tip: They pair well with beer!)

Try Myeongdong's Wide Selection of Street Treats!

Myeongdong is a lively district in Seoul (and this is where you can see more foreigners than Koreans). It offers a wide variety of tasty street food options that appeal to everyone's preferences. Whether you enjoy local flavors or international influences, you'll find something delicious to eat. As you walk around, you'll encounter enticing smells and food stalls, creating an **exciting culinary experience**!

1. **Bungeoppang 붕어빵** ("fish bread") features a crispy and sweet waffle-like batter that is traditionally filled with a sweet red bean paste. *Don't worry! It does not contain any actual fish.*

2. **Hotteok 호떡** is a sweet pancake-like treat filled with a sweet mixture consisting of brown sugar, cinnamon, and chopped nuts. The filled dough is flattened and cooked on a griddle until it becomes crispy on the outside, while the sugar filling melts and becomes gooey on the inside.

3. **Hoeori Gamja 회오리 감자** ("tornado potato") is made by taking a whole potato and spiraling it on a skewer, which creates a long, continuous spiral shape resembling a tornado. The potato is then deep-fried until it turns crispy and golden brown.

4. **Eomuk Kkochi 어묵꼬치** ("fish cake skewer") are made from a mixture of ground fish, flour, and various seasonings. They are particularly popular during the cold winter days in Korea."

Noryangjin Cupbap Street
노량진 컵밥 거리
Dongjak-gu, Noryangjin-ro 178
동작구 노량진로 178

5 min walk (0.19 miles / 314 m) from
Noryangjin Station Exit #8 Subway Line 1 or 9

SCAN FOR DIRECTIONS!

Try Cupbap - "Meal in a Cup", a Popular Choice among Students!

Cupbap 컵밥 ("meal in a cup") has become a popular choice among **students in *Gosichon*** (village of students preparing for civil service exams) due to its affordability. However, as word spread about its cost-effectiveness, the general public started visiting as well, resulting in a trend and the emergence of dedicated Cupbap streets. Experience a delicious and reasonably priced meal in a cup!

Dream High blog.naver.com/oliveras (CC BY-ND 2.0 KR)

Explore a Variety of Meal Boxes Available at Convenience Stores!

With an increasing number of young people living alone, **convenience store meal boxes** are gaining popularity. These affordable products offer excellent quality, making them a great choice to try! Different chains carry different products, so don't stop after just one!

Souvenir Shoppin

Seoul's vibrant souvenir shops and flea markets offer an incredible selection of unique and traditional Korean souvenirs. From traditional crafts to modern trinkets, these shops offer something for everyone.

SCAN FOR DIRECTIONS!

Insadong Ssamzi Gil 인사동 쌈지길
Jongno-gu Insadong-gil 44
종로구 인사동길 44

5 min walk (0.19 miles / 304 m) from
Anguk Station Exit #6 Subway Line 3

It's a popular shopping mall among tourists looking for **traditional Korean crafts** and **art with a modern spin**. This unique 4-story spiral building hosts **more than 70 shops and galleries**. Visitors can explore a wide range of items with diverse designs that are inspired by Korean traditional elements. The distinctive layout of the building, with the floors interconnected like an alleyway (hence the name "*gil*," which means "street" in Korean), creates a delightful atmosphere.

4 Fashion, Miscellaneous Goods, Tea Houses, etc

3 Fashion, Clothing & Accessories Shops

2 Designer Art Products, Food, etc

1 Traditional Crafts, Food, etc

B1 Craft Studios, Restaurants, etc

B2 The Witch's Garden

JH blog.naver.com/rei_sunshine (CC BY-ND 2.0 KR)

How Many of the Building's Symbol Can You Find?

The letter "ㅆ" is a consonant in the Korean alphabet and is the **first sound of the word "Ssamzi"**! For this reason, it is the logo for the building. As you explore the building, you'll find this letter randomly placed in different spots. How many can you find?

Find the Iconic Korean Totem Poles!

민트호수 blog.naver.com/snropro (CC BY 2.0 KR)

As you stroll through the shops, you will come across *Jangseung* 장승, which are **Korean totem poles**. Traditionally, these wooden structures were positioned at the outskirts of villages to designate village boundaries and ward off evil spirits. Look for the *Jangseungs* standing guard at the stores, alongside miniature versions that have been transformed into gift items!

Enjoy Art and Burn Some Calories at the Same Time!

As you take the stairs located left to the main entrance, the walls are adorned with a captivating "**Stairway Gallery**." Numerous paintings grace the space, inviting you to pause and immerse yourself in the artists' creations, all free of charge!

Insadong Street 인사동 거리

The streets surrounding Ssamzi-gil building are filled with antique / souvenir shops and tea houses.

Discover the Beauty of Smile Engraved In Traditional Masks!

Tal Bang 탈방
Jongno-gu, Insadong-gil 48
종로구 인사동길 48

Everyday 11 a.m. - 7 p.m.
SUN CLOSED
gahoemuseum.org

This unique boutique specializes in **traditional Korean masks**, offering a wide range of beautiful products, including large masks for your walls and cute mask badges to enhance your outfits. Explore and experience the beauty and craftsmanship of these authentic Korean masks.

Do the Iconic Dalgona Challenge!

Have you seen Squid Game? If so, you probably know the concept! Seek out a store that sells *dalgona* 달고나 candy and skillfully break it into a predetermined shape without shattering the entire piece!

탈만든이 blog.naver.com/sandaemas (CC BY 2.0 KR)

This is a one-of-a-kind **stamp shop** where customers can create their own **unique stamps** for someone special, and they can be personalized with different designs and phrases. They also offer calligraphy products for sale.

Saegim Sori 새김소리
Jongno-gu, Insadong-gil 55-1 종로구 인사동길 55-1

MON - SAT 10 a.m. - 6 p.m.
SUN CLOSED

딸기맘양갱이
blog.naver.com/parkyang102
(CC BY 2.0 KR)

추지 blog.naver.com/chu4246 (CC BY-SA 2.0 KR)

Guem Ok Dang 금옥당
Jongno-gu, Insadong-gil 49
종로구 인사동길 49

MON - SUN 10:30 am - 8:30 pm

This is a *yanggaeng* 양갱 (sweet red bean jelly) specialty store, a dessert/snack that Koreans love. It is made by preparing the red bean paste directly in a cauldron with fresh domestic red beans. It is also popular as a gift set due to its beautiful packaging.

Hwanghakdong Flea Market 황학동 벼룩시장 Jung-gu Majang-ro 5-gil 11-7 중구 마장로5길 11-7
6 min walk, (0.24 mi / 392 m) from **Sindang Station EXIT #11 Subway Line # 2 OR 6**

EVERYDAY 10 a.m. - 6 p.m.

The market emerged in the early 1970s when street vendors began selling used goods and antiques in the area. Over time, the market grew and became a **hub for antique collectors** and **bargain hunters**. It gained popularity for its diverse range of merchandise, including antique furniture, ceramics, traditional Korean artwork, vintage clothing, and various other unique items, earning the nickname **"all-things market"**. Antique collectors especially love it because they can find valuable items at lower prices if they're lucky.
Try haggling for an even better deal!

Antique shops provide an exciting chance to explore the past and delve into the lifestyles of various countries. **Seek out an item that represents a bygone aspect of Korean society**, something that is no longer relevant in today's modern Korean culture. Who knows? You might be the one to uncover a hidden gem during your search!

There are numerous places where you can find **high-quality clothes at incredibly low prices**! Some places even offer clothes sold by weight, which means you pay based on the weight of the items you choose. The value you can get at these places is truly unbeatable.

GANGNAM STYLE
EXPLORE KOREA'S TRENDIEST DISTRICT!

Immerse yourself in the vibrant culture of Gangnam, the **trendiest** and **fashionable** part of Seoul, through a variety of fun activities and experiences. From trying out the latest K-beauty trends to indulging in delicious local cuisine, you'll get to see and do it all.

MAP OF LOWER SEOUL

Gangnam 강남, meaning "region south of Hangang," is often associated with the affluent area of Seoul consisting of three districts, **Gangnam-gu 강남구**, **Seocho-gu 서초구**, and **Songpa-gu 송파구** and is known for its high house prices and concentration of wealthy individuals. Gangnam is renowned for its luxury boutiques, high-end department stores, and extensive infrastructure. Owning an apartment in Gangnam is seen as a symbol of success, although people living there are sometimes portrayed as materialistic in Korean pop culture.

1 **COEX 코엑스**

Gangnam-gu Yeongdong-daero 513 강남구 영동대로 513
Directly connected from **Bongeunsa Station Exit #7 Subway Line 9**

COEX Convention 10 a.m. – 6 p.m.
Starfield COEX Mall 10:30 a.m. – 10 p.m.

SCAN FOR DIRECTIONS!

COEX, short for "Convention and Exhibition," is a massive complex, including a convention and exhibition center, a large underground mall called Starfield COEX Mall, three luxury hotels, a cinema, and an Aquarium. The mall is the biggest underground mall in Asia and offers everything you need for entertainment and shopping.

Locate the Statue Depicting the Iconic Dance of the K-Pop Mega Hit Song - Gangnam Style!

When the song "Gangnam Style" became a worldwide sensation in 2012, everyone sang and danced along to the catchy line "Oppa Gangnam Style!" while doing the famous horse-riding dance. In celebration of K-Pop's global success, a statue depicting the iconic dance move, with two hands crossed, was erected at the entrance of the Starfield Mall. Go ahead and do the horse-riding dance!

Discover a Captivating Haven for Book Lovers!

Starfield Library 별마당도서관, situated in COEX Mall is a captivating and spacious library known for its impressive book collection. It features a towering 13-meter-tall bookshelf in a 2,800-square-meter atrium, providing a comfortable reading and studying environment with ambient lighting. The library boasts a diverse collection of around 70,000 books, covering various genres and languages, as well as magazines and e-books. It offers study tables with power plugs for laptop use and hosts a range of cultural events, including author talks, poetry readings, and literary concerts.

헛똑똑 blog.naver.com/ysc5258 (CC BY 2.0 KR)

---

2 **RODEO STREET 로데오거리**

Gangnam-gu Apgujeong-ro 46-gil 30 강남구 압구정로 46길 30
6 min walk (0.28 mi / 453 m) from **Apgujeong Rodeo Station Exit #5 Subway Line Suin-Bundang**

SCAN FOR DIRECTIONS!

Immerse Yourself In the Vibrant Youth Culture of Gangnam

Originally a hub of fashion and rebellion in the early 90s, this location attracted youth aiming to defy older norms. Once synonymous with opulent cars and high-end attire, it has transformed into a symbol of diverse youth subcultures and current trends. Upscale brands, skincare, plastic surgery, and hair salons populate the area. Alongside culinary delights and entertainment options, a range of dining establishments and cafes are available.

쵸묵쵸묵 어훙이 blog.naver.com/day265 (CC BY-SA 2.0 KR)

GALLERIA DEPARTMENT STORE
갤러리아백화점

Gangnam-gu Apgujeong-ro 343 강남구 압구정로 343
Directly connected from **Apgujeong Rodeo Station Exit #7
Subway Line Suin-Bundang**

SCAN FOR DIRECTIONS!

Experience Seoul's Premier Shopping Destination

A renowned and upscale shopping spot, this department store is celebrated for its exclusive brands, fashionable clothing, and distinctive designer selections. Shoppers relish a lavish and immersive experience. The food court presents an array of delectable dishes to savor. As night falls, the store adorns its outer walls with vibrant lights, crafting a breathtaking visual spectacle.

똘똘이양일상 blog.naver.com/woonga27 (CC BY-SA 2.0 KR)

4 GAROSU-GIL
가로수길

Gangnam-gu Apgujeong-ro 126 강남구 압구정로 126
12 min walk (0.34 mi / 553 m) **Apgujeong Station Exit #5 Subway Line 3**

SCAN FOR DIRECTIONS!

Visit the Trendiest Neighborhood in Seoul!

The name "tree-lined avenue", came from the 160 ginkgo trees that stand in a straight line along the street, and the area became one of the trendiest neighborhood in Seoul lately. It used to be a hub for galleries and designer shops, but the current trend is focused on various fashion shops. Additionally, you'll find charming cafes and restaurants to enjoy along the way.

꿈꾸는여행 도도 blog.naver.com/travelerdodo (CC BY-SA 2.0 KR)

Find the Trees Wearing Cute Sweaters!

When you visit in winter, you'll see something cute - the trees are wearing different sweaters to keep them warm! Find your favorite design and take a picture!

나나망고 blog.naver.com/televisiky
(CC BY-SA 2.0 KR)

CENTRAL CITY
센트럴시티

Seocho-gu, Shinbanpo-ro 176 서울 서초구 신반포로 176
Directly connected from **Express Bus Terminal Station Exit #3**
Subway Line 3 / 7 / 9

SCAN FOR DIRECTIONS!

This mega-complex offers a wide range of amenities, including the JW Marriott hotel, an express bus terminal, subway lines 3, 7, and 9, Shinsegae department store, Megabox cinema, a bookstore, and Famille Station with its array of restaurants. As one of Seoul's busiest spots, it provides plenty of activities and attractions. Don't forget to explore the underground stores for great bargains and discounts.

Pectus Solentis via Wikimedia Commons (CC BY-SA 2.0)

SCAN FOR DIRECTIONS!

Explore Korea's Busiest Department Store!

This department store is not just big, with 11 floors and many different stores, but it was also the top-ranking global department store in terms of sales in 2021. However, the real highlight here is the fantastic food you can find at the food court and underground mart, where you can even buy local groceries. Located near the Express Bus Terminal, this place is always bustling with people, giving you a true taste of Seoul's vibrant and lively atmosphere.

Visit the Beautiful Rooftop Garden to Enjoy a Refreshing Atmosphere!

Go to the 11th floor of Shinsegae Department Store and visit the "S Garden," a rooftop garden where you can take a peaceful break surrounded by pretty flowers and grass. It's like a little oasis in the middle of the city, perfect for refreshing your tired mind. The garden also has different exhibitions every few months, so there's always something new to discover and enjoy during your visit.

안수지 blog.naver.com/suziesuzie (CC BY-SA 2.0 KR)

GOTO MALL 고투몰

Walk towards **Exit 8-1 / 8-2** at **Express Bus Terminal Station** Subway Line 3 / 7 / 9

Everyday 10 a.m. - 10 p.m.

Goto Mall 고투몰, located below Gangnam Express Bus Terminal, is a vast underground shopping mall in with a diverse selection of products, including clothing, cosmetics, accessories, home decor, crafts, and flowers. You can shop rain or shine, and the mall's subway connection makes it convenient to travel anywhere. The best part is that you can find fantastic deals at prices much lower than department stores!

탁가이버 blog.naver.com/tacgyber (CC BY-SA 2.0 KR)

6 KAKAO FRIENDS 카카오프렌즈

Seocho-gu Gangnam-daero 429 서초구 강남대로 429
2 min walk (0.07 mi / 120 m) **Gangnam Station Exit #10 Subway Line 2**

Everyday 10:30 am - 10 pm

Meet Korea's Most Beloved Characters - Kakao Friends!

프리한자유
blog.naver.com/ijj0324 (CC BY-SA 2.0 KR)

KakaoTalk is a popular chatting app virtually everyone uses in Korea, partly because of the adorable characters it has. This shop offers a chance to interact with these cute characters and purchase souvenirs. It's a must-see for KakaoTalk enthusiasts, and the rooftop cafe at the shop is also worth exploring for its impressive views.

7 GANGNAM SAMSUNG 강남 삼성

Seocho-gu Gangnam-daero 411 서초구 강남대로 411
1 min walk (0.03 mi / 50 m) **Gangnam Station Exit #10 Subway Line 2**

Mon - Sat 11 am - 9 pm / Sun 11 am - 7 pm

Explore the Latest Technology at Samsung's Showroom!

Discover the thrill of this recently launched flagship store. Delve into Samsung's rich history and explore cutting-edge innovations across four engaging levels. Engage in interactive games, explore diverse products, capture moments at "photo spots," and relax in the cozy lounge. Enjoy free phone charging stations, especially useful for travelers. For the best experience, begin on the 4th floor and progress downwards.

쭈뉘 blog.naver.com/musicits (CC BY-ND 2.0 KR)
)

LOTTE WORLD TOWER

Songpa-gu Ollimpik-ro 300 송파구 올림픽로 300
2 min walk (0.05 mi / 80 m) from **Jamsil Station Exit #2**
Subway Line 2 & 8 (Also directly connected through underground path. Look for **"Seoul Sky Observation Deck"** sign.

Mon - Sat 11 am - 9 pm / Sun 11 am - 7 pm

SCAN FOR DIRECTIONS!

lwt.co.kr

This is an iconic skyscraper and a symbol of modernity and innovation. Soaring to a height of 555 meters (1,821 feet), it is one of the tallest buildings in the world. This architectural masterpiece houses a mix of commercial, residential, and entertainment spaces. From its observation deck on the upper floors, visitors can enjoy breathtaking panoramic views of the city. It offers a captivating blend of luxury, shopping, dining, and cultural experiences, making it a must-visit destination for locals and tourists alike.

Be the Tallest Person in Korea at the Sky Observatory Deck!

The Sky Observatory Deck at Lotte World Tower is a compelling attraction with numerous draws. It offers sweeping vistas of Seoul's landmarks and Hangang. The glass-bottomed SkyWalk provides excitement, complementing the tower's architectural feat. Amid multimedia displays, visitors can grasp Seoul's blend of tradition and modernity. Nighttime brings a captivating cityscape transformation. The deck presents a chance for cherished moments and deep engagement with Seoul's vitality.

seoulsky.lotteworld.com

Take a Stroll along the Seokchon Lake!

This lovely place features two artificial lakes, Seo-ho (west lake) and Dong-ho (east lake). Seo-ho is home to Lotte World's enchanting "Magic Island," while Dong-ho offers picturesque hiking trails and jogging paths along its shores. In 2014, it hosted the renowned "Rubber Duck" sculpture by Florentijn Hofman. Conveniently located near the Lotte complex, this peaceful park provides a serene escape. It is particularly cherished for its cherry blossoms during April and May.

OLYMPIC PARK
올림픽공원

Songpa-gu Ollimpik-ro 424 송파구 올림픽로 424
Mongchontoseong Station Exit #1 Subway Line 8

SCAN FOR DIRECTIONS!

Silas Low Wikimedia Commons (CC BY-SA 4.0)

Initially constructed for the 1988 Seoul Olympics, this expansive 408-acre park symbolizes Korea's modern advancement. It encompasses sports arenas, woodlands, and open lawns. The park is segmented into sections for recreational sports, cultural activities, eco-friendly zones, and historical encounters. Given its size, over three hours might be needed to fully explore, making it wise to review the park map beforehand!

Find Your National Flag at the Flags Square!

Seoul Olympic Park features the Flags Square, which displays the flags of all 200 countries participated in the 1988 Seoul Summer Olympic Games. Find the flag of your country and take a photo!

Visit the Artworks by World-Renowned Artists!

The finger sculpture is a bronze artwork created by Cesar Baldaccini, a renowned French sculptor, to commemorate Seoul's bid for the Olympics. Baldaccini crafted this sculpture in 1988. It is the world's only collection of seven large thumb sculptures, symbolizing the power of unity and achievement.

The sculpture 'Virtual Sphere' is located in Rose Square, and is a monumental work created by Venezuelan painter and sculptor Soto to honor Korea, the host country of the 1988 Olympics. It takes the form of a round object made of red and blue aluminum tubes, featuring the taegeuk 태극 pattern found in the Korean flag. Its exquisite beauty can be appreciated from all angles, resembling waves.

이형영 blog.naver.com/robot179 (CC BY-SA 2.0 KR)

K-POP ADVENTURE

Take a journey through Korea's music scene, where you'll get an up-close and personal look at the industry that has taken the world by storm. Visit K-Pop entertainment companies, follow the footsteps of K-Pop stars, take photos with the iconic K-Pop bear statues, and even learn a few dance moves to experience what it's like to be a K-Pop idol!

SCAN FOR DIRECTIONS!

Embark on a Pilgrimage to the 4 K-Pop Entertainment Giants!

1 **YG Entertainment** Mapo-gu, Hapjeong-dong 397-6 마포구 합정동 397-6
10 min walk (0.31 miles / 510 m) from **Hapjeong Station Exit #8 Subway Line 2 & 6**

Known for its famous artists and groups like **BIGBANG**, **BLACKPINK**, and **Winner**, YG unveiled its newly completed office building in 2020. The spacious facility boasts impressive features including a double-story auditorium, seven large dance practice rooms, seven recording studios, and 30 private music studios for exclusive composers and artists. Though **entry past the security gate is restricted**, the building's futuristic design speaks volumes about the artistic creativity nurtured within its walls!

the SameE 더세임카페 Mapo-gu, Hapjeong-dong 398- 마포구 합정동 398-21
Everyday 10 a.m. - 9 p.m.

SCAN FOR DIRECTIONS!

또져미 blog.naver.com/dlthwjd1224 *(CC BY-ND 2.0 KR)*

In front of YG's recently constructed headquarters, you'll find a vibrant cafe called "the SameE". The first and second floors are dedicated to **cozy cafe spaces**, while the basement level, B1, houses **merchandise shops featuring YG artists' products**. As a delightful bonus, there's a chance that **you might catch a glimpse of YG artists visiting the headquarters building** if luck is on your side!

2 **HYBE 하이브** Yongsan-gu, Hangang-daero 42 용산구 한강대로 42
10 min walk (0.32 miles / 530 m) from **Sinyongsan Station Exit #2 Subway Line 4**

SCAN FOR DIRECTIONS!

HYBE's new headquarters is a captivating hub for music production and content creation, serving as a central space for fans of artists like **BTS, TXT, NewJeans,** and **ENHYPEN**. While their previous auxiliary facility "**HYBE Insight**" offering exhibits and merchandise has ended, HYBE now hosts pop-up events at various locations, providing fans with unique experiences related to their artists and music. **Stay tuned for announcements from HYBE to learn about upcoming pop-up events and venues. Entry past the security gate is restricted.**

hybeinsight.com

수정다운 blog.naver.com/s99275 *(CC BY-ND 2.0 KR)*

3 **SM Entertainment** Seongdong-gu, Wangshimni-ro 83-21 성동구 왕십리로 83-21
3 min walk (0.03 miles / 58 m) from **Seoul Forest Station Exit #5 Subway Line Suinbundang**

SCAN FOR DIRECTIONS!

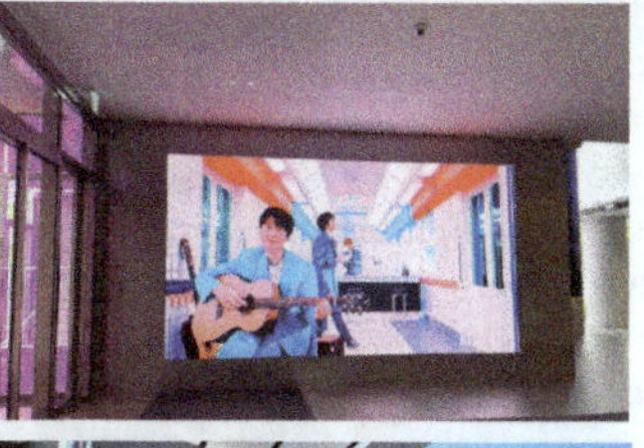

The new SM Entertainment headquarters building is located within D Tower. If luck is on your side, **you might have the chance to encounter popular SM celebrities** such as **Super Junior**, **NCT,** and **Aespa**. Even if you don't spot any celebrities, the neighborhood is still a delightful place to stroll, capture memorable photos, and potentially connect with fellow K-Pop enthusiasts who share the same passion. **Entry past the security gate is restricted**

KWANGYA Seoul 광야 서울 (B1 of SM Entertainment Building)

Everyday 10:30 am - 8 pm

KWANGYA is a **unique establishment** operated by **SM Entertainment**, offering not only **albums and merchandise** of their artists but also **a connection to the metaverse**. Within the **exhibition space**, scanning a QR code grants access to a **docent program**, enhancing the visitor's experience. Additionally, a zone utilizing transparent LEDs creates a captivating **three-dimensional ambiance**, simulating a concert hall with a range of vivid images. With its meticulous design and immersive features, it is a **must-visit destination** for international K-Pop fans.

1 Million Dance Studio 원밀리언 댄스 스튜디오
Seongdong-gu, Seongsu-dong 2-ga 322-2 성동구 성수동2가 322-2

SCAN FOR DIRECTIONS!

1MILLION Dance Studio welcomes students of all backgrounds and ages, **regardless of experience**. Their facility houses two fully equipped studios, and the staff is bilingual in English and Korean. Here, you have the opportunity to explore your creative potential and **master some of the iconic K-Pop dance moves**. To book an in-person class, simply visit their website.

④ JYP Entertainment Gangdong-gu, Gangdong-daero 205 강동구 강동대로 205
15 min walk (0.62 miles / 1 km) from **Dunchon Oryun Station Exit #1 Subway Line 9**

In 2018, JYP Entertainment moved from its previous office building in Cheongdam-dong to a new headquarters near Olympic Park. The new headquarters offers various amenities, including **practice rooms**, **recording studios**, and an **organic cafeteria**, impressing K-Pop fans and highlighting JYP Entertainment's commitment to providing top-quality facilities for their artists and staff. **Entry past the security gate is restricted.**

Follow the Footsteps of Your Favorite K-Pop Stars!

⑤ K-Pop Square Media Gangnam-gu Yeongdong-daero 513 강남구 영동대로 513
Right off **Samseong Station Exit #6 Subway Line 2**

Experience the awe-inspiring spectacle of a venue adorned with a **massive screen**, four times the size of a basketball court, broadcasting an array of **captivating videos**. This remarkable space showcases not only dynamic three-dimensional advertisements but also music videos of beloved K-Pop idols. You can **take memorable photos**, while eagerly anticipating the appearance of their favorite artists on the screen. It's an immersive setting that seamlessly blends **media art**, **entertainment**, and an inviting atmosphere for all to enjoy.

⑥ K-Star Road 케이스타로드
Gangnam-gu, Apgujeong-ro 507-gil ⟷ Gangnam-gu, Dosan-daero 101-gil 6
강남구 압구정로 507길 ⟷ 강남구 도산대로 101길 6
18 min walk (0.74 miles / 1.2 km) from **Apgujeong Rodeo Station Exit #2 Subway Line Suinbundang**

똥뻬미
blog.naver.com/dhraldls
(CC BY-ND 2.0 KR)

Gangnam, known for Psy's "Gangnam Style," is where K-Pop culture originated. It's a trendy area in Korea, home to more than half of the country's entertainment agencies and the birthplace of many K-Pop stars. Here, you'll find **K-Star Road**, a **street created to celebrate this culture**. It features **18 bear-shaped statues** called **Gangnam Dols**, representing **popular K-Pop stars**.

Find All 18 Gangnam Dolls along the K-STAR ROAD!

소셜원헤드헌터김윤팔
blog.naver.com/hnet23
(CC BY2.0 KR)

GANGNAMDOL	2PM	MISSA	BTS	GIRLS GENERATION	INFINITE
4MINUTE	FT ISLAND	CNBLUE	EXO	B1A4	KARA
SUPER JUNIOR	SHINee	TVXQ	AOA	VIXX	BLOCK B

7 **Star Avenue Myeongdong 스타에비뉴 명동본점** Jung-gu, Eulji-ro 30, Lotte Department Store 1F
Between Metro Line 2 Euljiro 1-ga Station Exit #7, 8 and Lotte Hotel
중구 을지로 30 롯데백화점 명동본점 1층 (롯데백화점 / 롯데호텔 사이)

Everyday 9 a.m. - 6:30 p.m.

Meet the Digitally Recreated K-Pop Stars!

SCAN FOR DIRECTIONS!

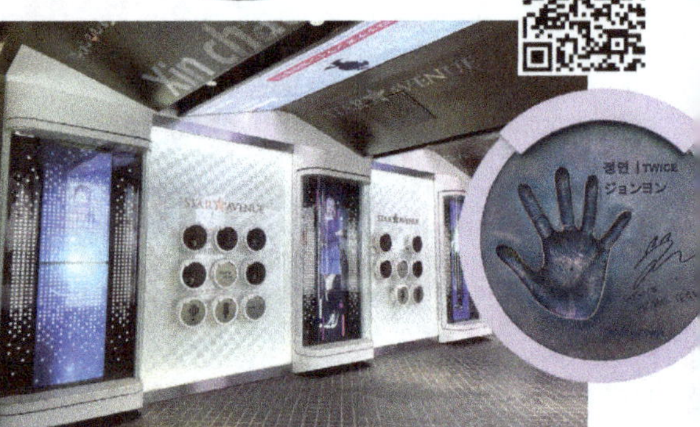

At this newly renovated space, you can meet the **digitally recreated K-Pop stars**. Walk through Star Track, a large-scale media tunnel, Star Mirror Zone, a mirror zone to take selfies with your favorite celebrities, and Hi-Five Zone, featuring hand printings of popular K-POP stars!

Get Your Favorite Idol's Merchandise at This Specialty Shop!

SCAN FOR DIRECTIONS!

MUSIC ART 뮤직아트
Jung-gu, Namdaemun-ro 67, B1 중구 남대문로 67 지하1층

Everyday 10:30 a.m. - 8 p.m.

This is the **ultimate destination for K-Pop goods**, featuring small-scale **exhibitions** and various **events** like pop-up stores and live performances. The shop also offers exclusive merchandise such as music video's behind-the-scenes photo books. It's a must-visit spot for K-Pop fans to connect with their favorite artists and discover unique products related to their music.

TRAGEDIES AND TRIUMPHS

EXPLORING KOREA'S HISTORY THROUGH MUSEUMS

Discover the **amazing achievements of the past** and learn about Korea's **modern history** and the struggles the nation faced. You'll hear both tragic stories and stories of victory that will leave you inspired and connected to the spirit of the Korean people. Jump on this unforgettable journey and celebrate the brilliance of the past and look forward to the future.

Learn the History of Divided Korea to Understand the Full Story!

1   **National Cemetery 국립 서울 현충원** Dongjak-gu Hyeonchung-ro 210 동작구 현충로 210
1 min walk (0.03 mi / 62 m) from **EXIT #8 Dongjak Station Exit #8 Subway Line 4 & 9**

This site holds the remains of more than **54,000 martyred patriots**, including soldiers, police officers, meritorious citizens, and key figures of the provisional government. It also **commemorates the 104,000 soldiers who died during the Korean War**, with many of their bodies still unfound. However, around 7,000 unknown soldiers' remains were discovered. Every year on June 6th, Memorial Day, the cemetery hosts memorial services and events to honor these brave individuals. The well-maintained cemetery offers **breathtaking scenery** and serves as both an informative historical destination and a lovely spot for a leisurely walk - a poignant reminder that freedom comes at a price.

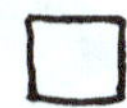

SCAN FOR DIRECTIONS!

As you stroll through the cemetery, you'll come across a **special section dedicated to the unknown soldiers**, those brave souls whose bodies were never found or remained unidentified. Pause for a moment of reverence and pay tribute to the unwavering spirit of these patriots who selflessly sacrificed their lives for their country.

2

> **War Memorial 전쟁기념관** Yongsan-gu, Itaewon-ro 29 용산구 이태원로 29
> 4 min walk (0.17 mi / 262 m) from EXIT #12 from **Samgakji Station Exit #12 Subway Line 4 & 6**

Everyday 9:30 a.m. - 6 p.m. Closed on Monday (If a national holiday falls on a Monday, it's closed the following day)

SCAN FOR
DIRECTIONS!

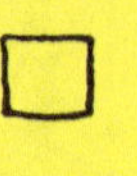

The War Memorial Museum was built in 1994 by the War Memorial Service Korea Society to honor the heroes who sacrificed their lives in the Korean War. This museum is vast and holds **over 33,000 artifacts**, with about 10,000 of them displayed in **five indoor and outdoor halls**. The museum's exhibitions show the most tragic and important part of Korean history, but they are also amazing and well thought-out. You'll be astonished by **how Korea transformed during that time**. It's a must-visit place!

www.warmemo.or.kr

As you stand in the memorial, you notice that it goes beyond remembering modern wars in Korea. Among the exhibits is a meticulously crafted scale model of the *geobukseon* 거북선, the legendary "Turtle Ship." This awe-inspiring vessel, invented by **Admiral Yi Sun-sin** during the Joseon Dynasty, played a pivotal role in the defeat of the Japanese navy during the late 16th-century Imjin War. Take a moment to closely examine this innovative ship and imagine what it must have been like to fight aboard such a historic and formidable vessel!

3

National Museum of Korea 국립중앙박물관 Yongsan-gu, Seobinggo-ro 137 용산구 서빙고로 137
3 min walk (0.19 mi / 308 m) from EXIT #2 from **Ichon Station Exit #2 Subway Line 4**
M/T/TH/F/SU - 10 a.m. - 6 p.m. (Last admission 5:30 p.m.) W/SA - 10 a.m. - 9 p.m. (Last admission 8:30 p.m.)

SCAN FOR DIRECTIONS!

The National Museum of Korea is a beloved **treasure trove** that holds the essence of Korean history and culture. It has an impressive collection of **420,000 items that span thousands of years**, from ancient hand axes to colorful gold crowns, celadon pottery, historical paintings, and modern photographs. The museum also offers **realistic videos and virtual reality experiences** to make the visit even more exciting.

www.museum.go.kr

Give the Kids a Unique Virtual Reality Experience!

For those with **children**, a must-see at the museum is the **Immersive Digital Gallery 2**. To enjoy this VR experience, you'll **need to make a reservation in advance**. The VR sessions run 12 times a day (16 times on Wednesdays and Saturdays), with each session lasting for 30 minutes, from 10:30 a.m. to 5:00 p.m. Due to high demand, reservations fill up quickly, especially during vacation periods. If you're planning to visit, be sure to check the reservation page for available dates and times. Sometimes, there may be 1 to 3 empty seats, providing a chance for last-minute reservations.

Find a Favorite Treasure from Each of the Different Dynasties and Kingdoms!

There were several dynasties and kingdoms in Korea throughout its history. Walk through the museum and **choose your favorite artifact from each dynasty and kingdom**. Then compare your choices with those of your friends!

4 **Seodaemun Prison History Hall 서대문 형무소** Seodaemun-gu, Tongil-ro 251 서대문구 통일로 251
6 min walk (0.16 mi / 250 m) from **EXIT #5 Dongnimmin Station Exit #5 Subway Line 3**
Everyday Mar - Oct 9:30 a.m. - 6 p.m. Nov - Feb 9:30 a.m. - 5 p.m. Closed on Monday
(If a National Holiday falls on a Monday, it's closed the next day.)

SCAN FOR DIRECTIONS!

www.sscmc.or.kr

Erected during the final years of the Korean Empire under the influence of the Japanese Empire, it stands as a testament to the years of **enduring hardships and national anguish in Korea's modern and contemporary history**. Remarkably, it serves as a poignant symbol of the anti-Japanese independence movement, reflecting the indomitable spirit of those who fought against Japanese oppression. Retaining its original form, it holds the memories of countless patriots who courageously resisted Japanese aggression. Visiting this historical site allows one to pay tribute to the sacrifices made by these Korean patriots and be inspired to walk in their footsteps.

Watch these Movies Before Visiting for Full Context!

Before visiting, it's highly recommended to watch several excellent movies/TV series that vividly portray the Japanese occupation of Korea and the Korean independence movement. These films offer valuable context and insight into the historical significance of the site. Here are some highly acclaimed ones to consider:

"The Age of Shadows" (2016)
"Assassination" (2015)
"Mr. Sunshine" (2018)

finding peace in seoul

A Spiritual Journey to Calm the Mind and Body

Delve into the heart of Korea's spiritual tapestry as you visit revered Buddhist temples, historic churches, and grand mosques. Immerse yourself in tranquil landscapes, embrace profound reflections, and find inner peace amidst cultural diversity.

1 **Jogyesa Temple 조계사** Jongno-gu Ujeongguk-ro 55 종로구 우정국로 55
7 min walk (0.31 mi / 508 m) from **Jonggak Station Exit #2 Subway Line 1**

Explore the Serenity of a Buddhist Temple!

Jogyesa Temple, the heart of Korean Buddhism, derives its name from **Jogyesan Mountain**, where Master Hyeneung once resided. A cultural treasure, the **Seated Buddha** graces the temple grounds. **Visitors are warmly welcomed 24/7 to the main hall.** In **spring**, witness the mesmerizing spectacle of countless **lotus lanterns** illuminating the temple, creating an enchanting sight not to be missed, both day and night.

Witness the Enchanting Lantern Parade!

Don't miss the vibrant **Lantern Festival** near Jogyesa Temple and Jongno streets, celebrating Buddha's birthday (April 4th, date changes every year as it's based on the Lunar Calendar).
A delightful spectacle for both locals and foreign tourists, the festival features various **events and parades** with colorful lanterns adorning the city. Over 100,000 lanterns illuminate the capital's main streets, culminating in the Lotus Lantern Parade's finale at Jogyesa. Immerse yourself in the festive spirit while celebrating Buddha's birthday at the Lotus Lantern Festival in the **Insadong area**, complemented by a visit to this revered temple.

2

Jongmyo Royal Shrine 종묘 Jongno-gu Hunjeong-dong 1 종로구 훈정동 1
3 min walk (0.19 mi / 299 m) **from Jongno 3(sam)-ga Station Exit #11 Subway Line 1 & 3 & 5**
Times change depending on season. Check the home page before visiting.

ROYAL PALACE PASS

Experience the Revered Legacy of Korean Heritage and Rituals

It is a **dignified Confucian sanctuary**, dedicated to the kings, queens, and descendants of the Joseon Dynasty. Surrounded by nature, it features halls and ritual preparation annexes. The shrine's simplicity and restrained decor create a solemn atmosphere for honoring ancestral spirits. The rituals hold great cultural significance, recognized by **UNESCO as "Masterpieces of Human Oral and Intangible Heritage"** since 2001 and listed as part of the **Intangible Cultural Heritage of Humanity since 2008**.

Take a Guided Tour for a Deeper Insight!

The shrine provides **guided tours** in **Korean**, **English**, **Japanese**, and **Chinese** on weekdays, each lasting approximately one hour. Guided tours in foreign languages are exclusively offered to foreigners and Koreans accompanying them. Check the homepage for details.

Myeongdong Catholic Cathedral 명동 성당 Jung-gu, Myeongdong-gil 74 중구 명동길 74
9 min walk (0.26 mi / 427 m) from **Myeongdong Station Exit #10 Subway Line 4**

Visit Korea's Birthplace of Roman Catholicism

The birthplace of the Roman Catholic Church community in Korea, offers a unique opportunity to delve into the rich religious and architectural history of the country. The impressive 23m high main building and 45m steeple, constructed with a variety of locally fired red and gray bricks, showcase the **blend of Korean and Western architectural influences**. The church's association with Emperor Gojong and the financial support from the Paris Foreign Missions Society adds to its cultural significance, making it a must-see destination for history enthusiasts and architecture lovers alike.

Attend an English Mass on Sunday!

mdsd.or.kr

Whether you're Catholic or not, attending a mass at this historic church offers a one-of-a-kind experience. An **English mass** is available every Sunday at 9 am.

Seoul Central Mosque 이슬람교 서울 중앙성원 Yongsan-gu, Usadan-ro 10-gil 39 용산구 우사단로 10길 39
10 min walk (0.30 mi / 477 m) from **Itaewon Station Exit #10 Subway Line 4**

koreaislam.org

Visit Korea's Birthplace of Islam!

The mosque was established with the dual purpose of serving as a **place of worship** for Muslims in Korea and as an **educational center** to promote understanding of Islam and Islamic cultures among the wider public. Inside the mosque, you'll find the Korea Muslim Federation office and a meeting room on the first floor. The men's musalla (prayer hall) is located on the second floor, while the women's musalla (prayer hall) is on the third floor. Both **worshippers and visitors are welcome to enter the mosque.**

Explore Halal Delicacies Around the Mosque!

Surrounding the mosque, there are **restaurants offering cuisine from various Islamic countries**. You can indulge in delightful halal dishes such as kebabs, shawarma, and Turkish delight, providing a sense of traveling to different nations while remaining within the same country!

Jeoldusan Martyrs Shrine 절두산 성지 Mapo-gu, Tojeong-ro 6 마포구 토정로 6
7 min walk (0.30 mi / 482 m) from **Hapjeong Station Exit #7 Subway Line 2 & 6**

Everyday 9:30 a.m. - 5 p.m. Closed on Monday

Explore the Site of Martyrdom and Faith!

jeoldusan.or.kr

Known as the **Decapitation Mountain**, this site witnessed a tragic prosecution of 1866, where up to **2,000 Korean Catholics lost their lives**, 27 of whom have been made **saints**. The museum beside the chapel displays some of the torture equipment from that time. Visited by **Pope John Paul II** in 1984 and **Mother Teresa** in 1985, it remains an inspiring place for all. **Sundays are the best time to visit, as many prayer gatherings take place on the grounds.**

SCAN FOR DIRECTIONS!

Michael Gallagher
flickr.com/michaelgallagher
(CC BY-SA 2.0)

Offer a Prayer Candle and Make a Wish!

The shrine features a dedicated section for **offering prayer candles**. Light a candle and make your heartfelt wish for your beloved ones.

6

Bongeunsa Temple 봉은사 Gangnam-gu Bongeunsa-ro 531 서울 강남구 봉은사로 531
1 min walk (0.08 mi / 135 m) from **Bongeunsa Station Exit #1 Subway Line 9**

Everyday 5 a.m. - 10 p.m.

Feel the Timeless Tranquility amidst Skyscrapers!

This 1,200-year-old temple was built in 794 during the Silla Kingdom. Despite surviving the suppression of Buddhism by the Joseon Dynasty, it later became **the main temple of the Korean Seon (Zen) sec**t from 1551 to 1936. Amidst modern skyscrapers, this tranquil temple provides a truly **inspirational contrast** in Korea.

Explore Ancient Buddhist Culture!

SCAN FOR DIRECTIONS!

bongeunsa.org

At the temple, a variety of activities await you, including the 2-day "**Temple Stay Program**" that offers an immersive monk experience. Enjoy **guided temple tours, lotus lantern making, meditation, Dado (tea-drinking ceremony), making salt Mandala, copying Sutra, 108 prostrations**, and **conversations with monks**, all conducted in **English**. For the most recent information, visit the homepage.

Whether you're a family looking to strengthen your bonds or a couple in search of romantic moments, Seoul has an abundance of excitement and **unforgettable experiences for everyone**. The city promises a delightful mix of family-friendly and intimate adventures that will surely create cherished memories to treasure.

1   **Namsan Seoul Tower 남산 서울타워** Jung-gu, Sopa-ro 83 서울 중구 소파로 83
13 min walk (0.31 mi / 508 m) from **Myeongdong Station Exit #3 Subway Line 4**
Everyday 10 a.m. - 11 p.m.

SCAN FOR DIRECTIONS!

nseoultower.co.kr

Visit the "Romantic Island" Of Seoul!

Standing tall atop (776.61 ft / 236.7 m) Namsan Mountain (859.58 ft / 262 m), this magnificent tower has earned the title of Seoul's **"Romantic Island"** in the heart of the city. Renowned for its everlasting allure, it offers a **stunning panoramic view of Seoul**. A symbol of the city itself, this tower holds the prestigious title of being the **top tourist attraction chosen by foreigners** and is revered as a **"sacred place" for couples**, who come to bask in the aura of eternal love.

Visit the 2nd Highest Toilet in Seoul!

Don't miss the opportunity to visit the **2nd highest toilet** in Seoul, located on the observatory's second floor! *Highest one is in Lotte World Tower.*

Below the Tower entrance, a heartwarming tradition awaits visitors, inviting them to **express their love by attaching a lock to a tree or fence**. Whether you choose to bring your own lock or find one at a nearby store, this touching gesture allows couples to symbolize their affection in a cherished manner. Even for those without a romantic partner, the love lock tree offers a chance to **reflect on the love shared with family**!

Seoul Education Research & Information Institute
서울특별시교육청 교육연구정보원
Jung-gu, Sopa-ro 46 중구 소파로 46

An **alternative route** to reach Namsan Tower is by taking the **stairs located near the Seoul Education Research Information Center**. Ascend the tall staircase, famously featured as a filming location in "My Name Is Kim Sam-soon," and follow the path to climb Namsan Mountain towards N Tower. As an exciting nod to the characters in the drama, consider trying the playful game of **rock-paper-scissors** to determine your climbing fate just as they did!

컬러램프지니
blog.naver.com/khjw0515
(CC BY-SA-KR 2.0)

SCAN FOR DIRECTIONS!

2 — **Itaewon World Food Street 이태원 세계음식거리**
Walk upthe alley beside **Hamilton Hotel**, and you'll find streets on either side lined with restaurants and bars. **Itaewon Station Exit #1 or #4 Subway Line 6**

SCAN FOR DIRECTIONS!

Itaewon is the **most diverse spot in Korea**, a global neighborhood where people from all around the world live together. This distinct area, **blending different cultures**, is cherished not just by foreign tourists, but also by Koreans wanting to **experience international culture within Korea**. Itaewon, with its contrasting day and night cultures, provides a **unique atmosphere unlike any other place in Seoul**!

Try Exotic Restaurants that are Non-Korean!

Itaewon World Food Street presents **a range of international cuisines**, occasionally tailored to suit Korean preferences, allowing you to enjoy even more **unique flavors**. Instead of picking a spot, take a stroll through the alleys for unexpected discoveries and surprises.

Go Bar Hopping to at least 3 Different Bars!

In Itaewon, **the night outshines the day**, attracting those seeking youthful enjoyment. Amid this lively scene, making new friends at creatively themed bars is especially exciting. Indulge in the distinct and entertaining bars of Itaewon!

Join the Annual Summer Pool Party!

Escape the heat and relish remarkable Itaewon views from the 5th-floor pool. Both locals and tourists flock here for people-watching, pool fun, and the social scene. Swimming, partying, and drinking are embraced – whether in the pool or at the bar atop **Hamilton Hotel**. Go for tanning, swimming, music from the DJ booth, burgers, and refreshing drinks.

hamilton.co.kr

Shop for Funny Korean Souvenirs!

While strolling, you'll come across street vendors offering **funny Korean souvenirs** like baseball caps and T-shirts with – perfect as playful souvenirs for friends back home!

Seoullo 7017 서울로 7017 Jung-gu Cheongpa-ro 432 중구 청파로 432
3 min walk (0.11 mi / 181 m) from **Seoul Station Exit #1 Subway Line 1 & 4**

SCAN FOR
DIRECTIONS!

Take a Walk in the Garden above the City!

Seoullo7017, also known as the **Seoul Skygarden**, is the fascinating result of an urban redevelopment project. It is an **elevated pedestrian walkway** that spans over a kilometer long, offering a unique and immersive experience for visitors. This beautifully landscaped pathway was once an old highway overpass but has been transformed into a green oasis, adorned with a variety of plants, flowers, and cultural installations. It provides a captivating glimpse of the city's **past** and **present** while offering **breathtaking views of the bustling streets below**.

Wait Until Sunset to Embrace the Night's Enchanting Ambience!

Seoullo 7017 undergoes a captivating transformation **at night**, offering a **completely different ambiance**. Wait until sunset to witness the mesmerizing difference and experience its enchanting charm!

Discover the Stone Post that marks its past!

As you stroll along the walkway, keep an eye out for a **stone post** labeled 서울고가 **(Seoul Elevated Road)** that bears testament to its historical significance. Discovering this landmark will truly enhance your appreciation of the remarkable transformation that has taken place here.

Cheonggyecheon 청계천 Jongno-gu Cheonggyecheon-ro 1 서울 종로구 청계천로 1
12 min walk (0.24 mi / 387 m) from **Dongdaemun Station Exit #6 Subway Line 1 & 4**

SCAN FOR
DIRECTIONS!

Explore Urban Oasis in the Middle of the City! ☐

Long ago, it was just an abandoned waterway. But a restoration project transformed it into a beautiful 7.0 mi / 10.9 km long park in the middle of Seoul. Now, it's like an **oasis in the city**, full of nature's beauty. There are **20 lovely bridges** that show how the past and future can be friends. It's a perfect place for a **relaxing walk**, **fun family time**, or a **romantic date night**.

Spot these Special Animal Guests! ☐

Occasionally, **herons** and **egrets** visit the stream, symbolizing the seamless blend of modern architecture and nature preservation achieved through the restoration project. However, spotting them **depends** on luck as their presence fluctuates with the seasons and environmental conditions.

Try Foot-Dipping to Cool Off! ☐

As the weather gets hotter in Seoul, more people are visiting the stream to cool off. **While foot-dipping is allowed, swimming and bathing are prohibited according to the city's ordinance!**

Enjoy the Iconic Statue with This Corn Chip for a Good Laugh!

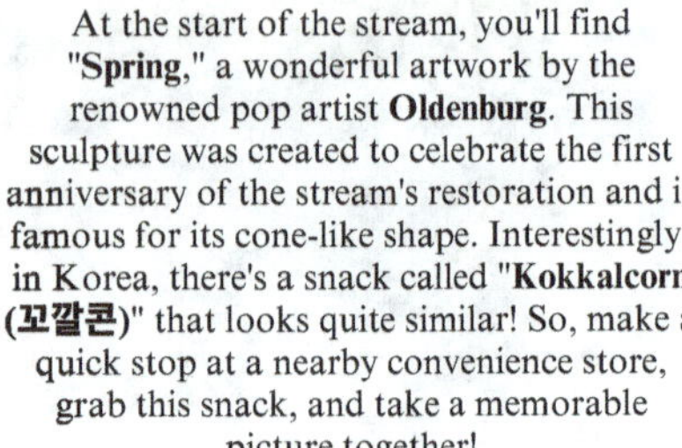

At the start of the stream, you'll find "**Spring**," a wonderful artwork by the renowned pop artist **Oldenburg**. This sculpture was created to celebrate the first anniversary of the stream's restoration and is famous for its cone-like shape. Interestingly, in Korea, there's a snack called "**Kokkalcorn (꼬깔콘)**" that looks quite similar! So, make a quick stop at a nearby convenience store, grab this snack, and take a memorable picture together!

---

④ Museum Kimchikan 뮤지엄 김치간
Jongno-gu, Insadong-gil 35-4, 4~6F 종로구 인사동길 35-4, 4~6층
5 min walk (0.23 mi / 344 m) from **Anguk Station Exit #6 Subway Line 3**
TUE - SUN 10 a.m. - 6 p.m MON, 1/1, Seollal, Chuseok, Christmas Closed

Learn Everything about Kimchi at This Amazing Museum!

museumkimchikan **kimchikan.com**

Nothing represents Korean culture more than *kimchi*! This museum offers a quick and comprehensive way to learn all about it. It was founded in 1986, then renovated and reopened on April 21, 2015, as "**Museum Kimchikan**." The museum is packed with both **real** and **digital exhibitions** focused on kimchi. There are interactive displays and attractions to enjoy on each floor from the 4th to the 6th.

No reservation needed for 20 people or less. Contact for larger groups.

Join The Kimchi-Making Experience!

Join this exciting **kimchi-making class** and **create your own kimchi to take home**! No need to worry about materials; everything will be provided. All are welcome, including children aged six and above. If plans change, inform **at least 4 days before your reservation**. Gather friends, as a **minimum of 5** participants are needed (they can accommodate **up to 24 participants per program**). So be part of this wonderful kimchi-making journey and immerse yourself in Korean culture!

Make a reservation in advance by emailing **museum@pulmuone.com**. Visit homepage for more info.

Daehak-ro 대학로
Jongno-gu, Jongno-5(o)-ga Station Exit # 1-8 ⟷ Jongno-gu, Daehak-ro 156
종로구 종로5가역 1 ~8 출구 ⟷ 종로구 대학로 156

Explore a Vibrant Playground for the Young at Heart!

Literally meaning "college street", it's known as the **hub of Korean performing arts**, is a concentration of small theaters. The name originated from the establishment of Gyeongseong Imperial University during the Japanese colonial era in 1922. After liberation, it became Seoul National University until it relocated, and the area retained the name Daehak-ro. Despite no longer having a university, it remains a **vibrant place for the younger generation**, offering a variety of **attractions**, **activities**, and **entertainment** that offer insights into their current trends and interests.

보현 blog.naver.com/qwd7882

Sing Your Heart Out at Coin Noraebang!

Coin *noraebang* (karaoke) **코인노래방** offers **affordable entertainment in a private room** with your friends because you can pay per song or use time-based passes with coins or credit cards! The rooms feature modern sound systems and touch-screen song selection. Easily found throughout Seoul, it's a favorite hangout for singing enthusiasts. **Songs are available in many languages**.

- 악쓰는하마 Jongno-gu, Daemyeong-gil 9, 3F 종로구 대명길 9, 3층
  EVERYDAY 12 p.m. - 2 a.m.

- 에코 Jongno-gu, Daemyeong-gil 40, B1 종로구 대명길 40, 지하 1층
  MON - THUR 9 a.m. - 4 a.m. FRI - SUN 9 a.m. - 6 a.m.

폰앤러브 blog.naver.com/hddpark7

Capture Your Happiest Moments in "4-cut photos"!

The "four-cut photo" trend is sweeping through popular neighborhoods, captivating Korean youth as the latest craze for capturing memories. **Affordable booths** offer various features like **props, changeable lighting**, and **Instagram-worthy decorations**!

- 인생네컷 Jongno-gu, Myeongnyun 2-ga 186-2
  EVERYDAY 24 hrs 종로구 명륜2가 186-2

- **Photoism Colored 포토이즘 컬러드**
  Jongno-gu, Myeongnyun 4-ga 46-1 종로구 명륜4가 46-1
  EVERYDAY 24 hrs

- 시현하다 Frame Jongno-gu, Myeongnyun 4-ga 22-1
  EVERYDAY 24 hrs 종로구 명륜4가 22-1

Play Fun Games and Enjoy Delicious Food at PC Bang!

A visit to a **PC bang 피씨방** ("room") is a must for any tourist seeking a unique and exciting experience, because they are not only perfect for playing games with your friends but also a decent dating spot! The best part is the **fantastic food selection**, ranging from instant noodles to well-prepared meals by the PC bang staff!

Try One of the Menus at PC Bang!

- **프리미엄 PC방** Jongno-gu, Daemyeong-gil 9
  종로구 대명길 9   **EVERYDAY 24 HRS**

- **이스포츠 PC방** Jongno-gu, Seonggyungwan-ro 12, 2F
  종로구 성균관로 12, 2층   **EVERYDAY 24 HRS**

Find Your Way to Great Fun at Escape Cafe!

Lily blog.naver.com/yujin_blog

Experience the excitement of Korea's **thrilling escape cafes**! Put your wit and teamwork to the test as you solve puzzles and challenges in immersive adventures with friends or family. Race against the clock to escape the room in a given time! You will have an unforgettable experience that will leave you craving more mystery-solving fun. Hurry, time's ticking!

- **Secret Chamber 시크릿챔버** Jongno-gu Myeongnyun 2-ga 21-18
  EVERYDAY 10 a.m. - 0 a.m.   종로구 명륜2가 21-18

- **Sherlock Holmes 셜록홈즈** Jongno-gu, Daehak-ro 10-gil 5, 4F
  종로구 대학로 10길 5, 4층
  MON - FRI 12 p.m. - 11 p.m. SAT - SUN 11 a.m. - 11 p.m.

- **Epilogue 에필로그** Jongno-gu, Daehak-ro 8ga-gil 48
  EVERYDAY 10 a.m. - 9:50 p.m.   종로구 대학로8가길 48

Discover the Joy of Free Busking at Marronnier Park

Marronnier Park 마로니에 공원 in Daehak-ro is renowned for its outdoor performance hall, which has served as the debut stage for numerous prominent singers and actors. It's a **beloved spot for diverse artists**, from amateur singers playing acoustic guitars on weekends to up-and-coming talents showcasing their skills. Various events like festivals, busking performances, and flea markets are held here, making it a vibrant cultural and artistic space.

SCAN FOR DIRECTIONS!

이슬한잔 blog.naver.com/photoc3

v회야v blog.naver.com/plysh
(CC BY 2.0 KR)

Ihwa Mural Village 이화 벽화 마을
Jongno-gu, Ihwa-dong 9- 413 종로구 이화동 9-413
14 min walk (0.47 mi / 763 m) from **HyehwaStation Exit #2 Subway Line 4**

This captivating location is the result of a government project to transform an underdeveloped neighborhood into an artistic area. The joint efforts of local residents, artists, students, and volunteers collaborated to paint **stunning murals**. You will find **unique alleys** and **charming cafes**, offering **breathtaking views of downtown Seoul**. Unfortunately, some murals have been removed due to complaints from residents about the increasing number of tourists. Tourists are encouraged to explore the village's picturesque alleys and cafes while being considerate of the tranquil residential areas.

SCAN FOR DIRECTIONS!

 To enjoy a more relaxed and pleasant visit, it is recommended to plan your trip on weekdays and avoid the crowds.

6 **Funny Saju 재미난조각가** Mapo-gu, Seogyo-dong 358-124, 2F 마포구 서교동 358-124 2층
8 min walk (0.33 mi / 546 m) from **Hongik University Station Exit #9 Subway Line 2**

02-325-4543   **EVERYDAY 12:30 p.m. - 11:30 p.m.**

ENG / CHN service providers available! Call for an appointment.

 융진 blog.naver.com/thdwodms233
(CC BY-ND 2.0 KR)

Tourists visiting Korea should experience *saju* 사주 readings, an ancient method using "the four pillars of destiny" to **predict fate and destiny based on birth moment**. A skilled *saju* reader interprets the eight characters associated with your birth, representing yin or yang energy and five primary elements, providing insights into various aspects of life and future. *Saju* is not blindly trusted but valued for entertainment and life advice. Additionally, couples can explore *Gunghap* 궁합, the **analysis of marital compatibility**, and discover if they are a good match. This cultural practice showcases the Korean fascination with unlocking fate and destiny. Whether seeking entertainment or life guidance, saju readings offer a unique glimpse into Korean culture and traditions.

Have your name and date of birth in the Lunar Calendar system, as well as the time of birth, ready before visiting!

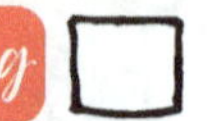
ispaland.co.kr

Relax and Recharge at a Korean Traditional Sauna - Jjimjilbang

SCAN FOR DIRECTIONS!

Korea's **traditional bathhouse**, *jjimjilbang* 찜질방, provides tourists with a **unique rejuvenating experience**, offering **themed saunas**, **hot tubs**, and **steam rooms**. It allows visitors to **immerse in Korean culture and relaxation**, with various **entertainment facilities for socializing and communal experiences**. including Families, couples, and friends often visit for a relaxing getaway, enjoying heated and steamed rooms, along with **restaurants, snack bars, fitness clubs, PC rooms, karaoke, nail shops, sports massages, arcades,** as well as **affordable overnight stays.**

Upon entering a jjimjilbang, you must change into the uniform they provide to maintain cleanliness and prevent contamination from any germs or viruses you might have brought in from outside.

Try Making the Korean "Lamb Head Towel Hat"

The *yangmeori* 양머리 "Lamb/Sheep Head" towel hat gained popularity after the main character wore it in the hit TV drama "My Name is Kim Sam-soon" in 2005. In jjimjilbang, people of all ages and genders use it to absorb sweat, keep their hair in place, and add a cute touch to their appearance!

Learn How to Make the Korean "Lamb Head Towel"!

Try at least 3 Different Sauna Rooms

마음자리 blog.naver.com/pej1425
(CC BY-SA-KR 2.0)

Explore the **various sauna rooms with different temperatures and health benefits**, such as the salt room, charcoal room, herb room, and jade room. Each room is said to offer a distinct experience and relaxation for your body.

Jjimjilbangs usually have both **sex-segregated** and **unisex** areas, with separate dressing and bathing rooms. The steam/sweat rooms and heated communal floors are often unisex but may vary between establishments.

Get the Korean Body Scrub for Baby-Smooth Skin!

In Korea, *ttaemiri* 때밀이 (body scrubbing) has been a **popular method for achieving smooth skin**. In many Korean public baths and jjimjilbangs, professional body cleansers offer complete shedding services. The process involves soaking the body in warm water to soften dead skin cells, followed by a thorough scrubbing using special towels and gloves.

복많이
blog.naver.com/hjwwworld
(CC BY-SA 2.0 KR)

Take a Power Nap on the Heated Floor!

Take a break from walking and sightseeing to relax in various resting areas, including **heated floors** and **reclining chairs**. Some *jjimjilbangs* offer **sleeping rooms** for napping or overnight stays, allowing visitors to recharge and refresh.

8 **Lotte World 롯데월드** Songpa-gu, Ollimpik-ro 240 송파구 올림픽로 240
2 min walk (0.09 miles / 145 m) from **Jamsil Station Exit #4 Subway Line 2 & 8**

Visit Lotte World for Unforgettable Fun for All Ages!

SCAN FOR DIRECTIONS!

This expansive entertainment complex draws in **more than 7 million visitors each year**, boasting the distinction of being home to one of the **world's largest theme parks**. Alongside its exhilarating rides, the complex offers a range of attractions including **shopping malls**, a **luxury hotel**, a **Korean folk museum**, **sports facilities**, and **movie theaters**. It's also home to **Korea's largest ice rink**. Throughout the park, **various performances** captivate visitors.

Lotte World is primarily divided into three sections:
Adventure - located on the indoor ground floor;
Underland - situated on the indoor underground floor;
Magic Island - outdoor artificial island

Ziggymaster
via wikimedia commons
(CC BY-SA 3.0)

Enhance your experience by downloading the **"Lotte World Adventure" app**, which provides information on show timings, ride wait times, closures, and maintenance. Additionally, it enables users to easily register physical tickets by scanning the QR code!

Experience the Theme Park in Korean School Uniform!

Rent and put on **Korean school uniforms** and have fun at Lotte World! It's a special way for foreigners to **feel like Korean students** and for Koreans to remember their past. Everyone, young or old, can enjoy it!

- **Gamsung Gyobok 감성교복** (Walk directly from the entrance of Adventure on the lower ground floor of Lotte World.)

Take a Pic in front of the Merry-Go-Round!

Taste the Iconic Gyro Churros!

If you're not feeling too brave, the shop offers delightful **churros** that **resemble Lotte World's famous "Gyro Drop" ride.**